# THEY SPEAK WITH OTHER TONGUES

# THEY SPEAK WITH OTHER TONGUES

By John L. Sherrill

HIGHLAND BOOKS

*They Speak With Other Tongues*

© 1964 by John L. Sherrill

Reproduced from the U.S. edition by arrangement
with Evelyn Singer Agency

*Tib*

# Preface

As soon as I joined our local church choir last fall, I realized I'd made a mistake. The beautiful anthems I'd enjoyed each Sunday were harder than they sounded! As my admiration for the rest of the choir rose, my view of my own musical gifts sank. I could not sight-read, my range was narrow, my volume puny. But the choir needed men's voices and the other members encouraged me, passing on tips on breath control, pitch, phrasing. Gradually my mind absorbed a little of this but the sounds that came from my throat were as unsatisfactory as ever.

Then one night at rehearsal I happened to take a chair directly in front of Bill Brogan. As the big Irishman's magnificent bass boomed forward, something quite remarkable happened to my own singing. I commented on it after rehearsal.

"If that helped," said Bill, "I'll show you something even better next week."

The following Thursday he took a seat next to me. Halfway through the Advent chorale he whispered, "Lean into me."

I looked at him, not understanding.

"Put your weight on me."

I still didn't understand, but I leaned back until my shoulderblade was resting on his chest.

And suddenly I knew what singing was all about. The resonances of his deep voice swelled through my own; effortlessly I made tones I hadn't known were in me.

It lasted only a short time, this moment of my virtuosity, but the incident impressed me doubly because it epitomized another such sequence in my life. Once before I had passed from intellectual inquiry, to the presence of the thing itself, and then on to something almost like physical contact. But that is the story of the book. . . .

*John L. Sherrill*

# Contents

# Chapter One

# The Leap

I still remember that I whistled as I strode up Park Avenue in New York City that spring morning in 1959, on my way to a follow-up visit at the doctor's. I stepped through the door of number 655 and nodded to the receptionist—she was an old friend by now. I'd been coming to Dr. Daniel Catlin's office every month since a cancer operation two years before, and it was always the same: the doctor's skilled fingers running down my neck, a pat on the back, "See you in a month."

But not that day. This time the fingers stopped, prodded, worked a long time. When I left I had an appointment at Memorial Hospital for surgery day after next.

What a difference in a spring morning! I walked back down the same street in the same sunshine, but now a cold, light-headed fear walked in me. I knew this fear; all cancer patients know it. But we keep it down, we stay on top of it with various mental tricks. Mine was the notion that one operation was all right, it was only if they called you back that you had to worry.

Now I could no longer hold the fear down. It rose up, scattering reason before it. I dove into the first church I came to, looking for darkness and privacy more than anything. It was St. Thomas Episcopal, on Fifth Avenue, and as I walked in the noon sirens were blowing. To my surprise a white-robed boys' choir was filing into stalls down in front and a few minutes later a young seminarian mounted the pulpit. A card in the pew told me I had stumbled into a Lenten noonday meditation.

I didn't know it then, but this brief address was to hold the key to the most astonishing experience of my life.

At the time it seemed wretchedly irrelevant to my problem. The young man gave a short talk on Nicodemus. Many of us try, he said, to approach Christ as Nicodemus did: through logic. "Rabbi, we know that you are a teacher sent by God," Nicodemus said, and then he gave his reason—a logical one: ". . . no one could perform these signs of yours unless God were with him." [1]

"But, you see," said the seminarian, "as long as Nicodemus was trying to come to an understanding of Christ through his logic, he could never succeed. It isn't logic, but an experience, that lets us know who Christ is. Christ, Himself, told Nicodemus this: 'In very truth I tell you, unless a man has been born over again he cannot see the kingdom of God.'" [2]

At the time, as I say, all this meant less than nothing to me. And yet the very next morning, I was to hear these same words again. My wife, Tib, and I were having coffee after a sleepless night, when the telephone rang. It was our neighbor, author Catherine Marshall LeSourd.

"John," she said, "could you and Tib get in the car and come over here for a few minutes? I've heard the news and there's something I've got to say to you."

Catherine met us at the door dressed in a housecoat, wearing neither make-up nor smile, which said more than words about the concern she felt. She led us into the family room, shut the door, and without polite-talk, began.

"First of all I want to say that I know this is presumptuous of me. I'm going to talk to you about your religious life, and I have no right to assume that it lacks anything. After all, you've been writing for *Guideposts* for ten years; you respect religion, you've studied it from many angles. But there is so much more to it than that . . ."

I looked at Tib: she sat still as a rock.

"John," said Catherine, "do you believe Jesus was God?"

It was the last question in the world I'd expected. I'd supposed she'd have something to say about God being able to heal, or prayer being a wonderful uplift when you're afraid—something to do with the crisis I was facing.

But she'd put the question to me; so I considered it. Tib and I were Christians, certainly, in the sense that we wrote "Protestant" on application blanks, attended church with some regularity, sent our three children to Sunday School. Still, I knew that these were habits: the fact was I had never come to grips with this very question, was Jesus of Nazareth, in fact, God? And now, when I tried, there were mountains of logic which halted me. I started to map them for Catherine, but she stopped me.

"You're trying to approach Christianity through your mind, John," she said. "It simply can't be done that way."

There it was again. Catherine went on. "It's one of the peculiarities of Christianity that you cannot come to it through intellect. You have to be willing to experience it first, to do something you don't understand—and then oddly enough, understanding often follows. And it's just that which I'm hoping for you today . . . that without understanding, without even knowing why, you say 'Yes' to Christ."

There was silence in the room. I had an eternity of reservations. And at the same time I had a sudden desire to do precisely what she was suggesting. The biggest reservation of all, I stated frankly: it just didn't seem right to shy away all these years and then come running when I had cancer and was scared and had my back to the wall.

"I'd feel like a hypocrite," I said.

"John," said Catherine almost in a whisper, "that's pride. You want to come to God in *your* way. When you will. As you will. Strong and healthy. Maybe God wants you now, without a shred to recommend you."

We talked for perhaps half an hour more, and when we left I still had not brought myself to make that step that was apparently all-crucial. A few moments later, however, just as the car was passing a certain telephone pole on Millwood Road in Chappaqua, a pole which I can point out to this day, I turned to Tib and said aloud,

"What do they call it: 'a leap of faith'? All right, I'm going to make the leap: I believe that Christ was God."

It was a cold-blooded laying down of my sense of what was logical, quite without emotional conviction. And with it went something that was essentially "me." All the bundle of self-consciousness that we call our ego seemed somehow involved in this decision. It was amazing how much it hurt, how desperately this thing fought for life, so that there was a real kind of death involved. But when it was dead and quiet finally, and I blurted out my simple statement of belief, there was room in me for something new and altogether mysterious.

The first hint that there was something different about me came rather inelegantly at the hospital. Shortly before the operation a snappy young nurse came in to give me an injection. Since Army days I have had a morbid horror of needles, whether wielded by pretty girls or not. Yet this time it aroused no terrors at all.

"All right, let's turn over," said my nurse in her most professional tone. But when she had finished, her tone changed. "My, you're the relaxed one! You act like you're here on your vacation."

It wasn't until after she had left that I realized how true and how curious this was. I *was* relaxed, deeply and truly, and lying in my hospital bed I began to suspect that something very remarkable was happening to me. It was as if in some secret and undefined part of myself I knew that, no matter how this operation turned out, it was only an inconvenience in an existence that was new and strange and quite independent of hospitals and surgeons, illness and recovery.

A little later some orderlies came in and I was taken out of my bed and put on a stretcher. I remember the orderlies' faces looking down at me, and a crack in the corridor ceiling gliding past overhead. The fluorescent light in the mammoth elevator wasn't working properly; it blinked on and off. Then there were other lights, blinding ones directly overhead, and out of them appeared the green-capped face of Dr. Catlin. I smiled at him and he smiled back and asked if I were ready.

"Ready and waiting."

There was another injection, and it seemed only an instant before I was awake again, in a room I had never seen before. It was night-time. I had gone into the operating room at eight o'clock in the morning. Why had it taken so long? Rubber pipes were sticking out of both sides of my chest, and out of a hole in my throat. Some sort of machine whirred and gurgled out of sight behind the bed.

And pain. The worst I had ever known. It was in my chest, where the pipes were. A nurse, seeing that I was awake, came over and took my pulse. I tried to talk but could not. I gestured wildly at the pipes.

"Doctor will see you in the morning. Try to get some sleep."

I would like to be able to say that—having made my leap of faith—those hours in the recovery ward were a triumph of soul over body. They were not. Pain demoralized me completely. Something had gone wrong on the operating table, and I was not practiced enough in the Christian life to find much else to think about.

In the morning I woke up in still another room. Bit by bit I pieced together the ceiling and window and sliding curtains of my original hospital room. The pipes were still sticking out of my chest and throat, machines still bubbling away somewhere behind my bed. But at least I got a little information. Dr. Catlin came to see me. He leaned over the bed, and in my half-conscious state I caught the words:

"You're doing fine now. There was a little trouble on the operating table. Lungs collapsed. Tracheotomy. Everything on your neck looks good, though. Get some rest now."

For another day I lay semi-drugged on the bed, aware occasionally of a visit from my wife, or my mother, or the doctor. Toward the end of the second day I became aware, too, of other patients in the room. One was an older man who was having a lot of trouble with a cough. Another was a youngster, who had also just come down from the recovery room and was in pain.

That night for the first time I was able to think about praying. I tried talking to this Christ I had stated a belief in, but it was like talking into the air over my bed. In no sense was there a feeling that I was in contact with anybody. I was worried about my roommates, the man with the cough and the boy in pain. I tried praying for them, but nothing happened. After a while I drifted into sleep, aware more than anything else that each of us in that room was very much alone.

It was the middle of the night, and I was awake. Fully awake, without transition from sleep. A little light came in from the hall, and from the windows. A nurse passed the door on rubber-soled shoes. Both of my roommates were restless, the one coughing, the other moaning softly.

I don't know how it was that I first became aware of the light. It was there, without transition, as my awakening had come. It was different from the light that came in through the door and window: more of an illumination than a light with a defined source. But there was something remarkable about this light: it had, somehow, a center of awareness. I was awed, but not at all afraid. Instead there was a sense of recognition as if I were seeing a childhood friend, physically much changed so that what I recognized was a totality rather than a particular feature.

"Christ?" I said.

The light moved slightly. Not really moved: it was just suddenly closer to me without leaving where it was. I thought for a moment that the pain beneath my bandages was going away, but it did not. Something happened with that encounter, though. It was as if I were bursting with health through and through.

My roommates were still tossing, still coughing and groaning. "Christ," I said moving my lips only, "would you help that boy?" The light did not leave me, but in some strange way it was now at the bedside of the boy in pain. A little "Ohhh . . ." came from him and he was silent.

"And my other friend?" The light was instantly centered on the bed of the old man who was in the middle of a spasm of coughing. The cough stopped. The old man sighed and turned over.

And the light was gone.

I lifted my head as far as I could from the pillow and searched the room but there was only the yellow light from the hall and the window. The nurse came back down the hall. A car honked, outside in the night. The machinery behind my bed whirred and wheezed. Everything was as it had been. Except that, lying there in a bed in Memorial Hospital, with bandages around my head and neck and chest, with pain still slicing through me, I was filled with a sense of well-being such as I had never known. I cried for a long time, out of joy.

I stayed awake until dawn, thinking that perhaps the extraordinary light would return. All that while my two roommates slept quietly. When the morning nurse came in with the tray of thermometers, she found me still awake.

"You look rested," she said.

"I am."

She turned to my roommates. "Well that's good. And they're both sleeping. I think I'll do this room later."

I was out of the hospital a full week earlier than Dr. Catlin had predicted, so rapidly did my body mend.

For several days after I returned home I tried to tell Tib about the encounter in the hospital. But to my embarrassment every time I opened my mouth to begin the same thing happened: I'd feel tears rush to my eyes and know that if I said one more word I'd be weeping like a child. It was only when I decided that Tib would have to know about the experience, tears or no, that I managed to get it out.

"Do you think it was a dream?" I asked, when I'd rather soggily finished.

"I don't believe a dream could affect you this way."

"Neither do I."

There were two other people I felt should hear the story, Len and Catherine LeSourd. I warned them that the experience might be difficult to talk about, and sure enough the same phenomenon repeated itself: I started off matter-of-factly and halfway through choked up.

"You see what you're in for?" I said, trying to laugh off my embarrassment.

But Len said, "It's those tears, John, more than anything else that make the thing real to me. Take your time."

So I told them. "And did you see the light again?" Catherine asked when I was through.

"No."

"I don't think you should expect to, either," she said. "This kind of face to face meeting with Christ usually happens just once. It happened to me in a way very like yours. With Len it was entirely different. But it's that certain recognition of Christ that's the amazing thing, however it happens."

And then Catherine said an interesting thing. As it turned out, it was a kind of prophecy. "I'm glad you told us. It will help fix it in your own mind, for the time when it no longer seems real." She smiled a little wistfully. "I wish there were some way to feel always as you do now. As far as I know, there isn't. Once we lose the freshness of that first meeting, we just have to walk by faith."

It took me a while to understand what she meant. Then and for weeks afterwards I lived in the glow of that encounter. The report from the doctor, when it finally came, was encouraging as far as the cancer went. But I found to my surprise that it didn't matter as much as I had expected. Something more engrossing occupied my mind. I wanted to get to know this Christ I had met.

For a while it was easy, thinking often about Him. It happened automatically, in fact. Reading the Bible was a brand new experience, because I could understand for the first time a lot that had puzzled me. How Jesus, for instance, could have recruited disciples simply by saying, "Follow me." That was easy to believe now: that Presence I'd felt was something you'd follow to the ends of the earth. The stories of healing were like reliving that night in the hospital. John's statement, "God is love," was for me now a description rather than a principle.

But, as the weeks, and then the months passed, the first sharpness faded. After a while, it was not quite so easy to pick up the Bible; going to church slipped back slowly, yet certainly, into routine; and one day, visiting a friend in the hospital, I told him about my experience and got through the recital dry-eyed. That, more than anything, convinced me that what I had was a memory, no longer a living reality.

And was this all, now, that I would ever have? I felt a little as the disciples must have felt when, after Christ had walked beside them for a time, He was suddenly gone. I felt a deep sadness, a yearning to get back in touch with Him but, as

Catherine had predicted, there was nothing much I could do about it except to "walk in faith."

In talking with other Christians I found that this was a very, very common experience. There was a mountain-top meeting, a period when the reality of Christ was unmistakable, and then a slow drifting away. There was a brief moment of intense love, of joy and deep-running peace, a period of real wholeness when without straining for self-control you found that you were patient, kind, gentle. It was a time of believing. And then a dull dryness took over.

Was this the way it was meant to be? Were believers supposed to live on a memory? I somehow doubted it: memories fade and become confused.

And then, about a year after that hospital encounter, I met a man who told me an intriguing story. It caught my attention at first simply because it was so bizarre. Certainly I did not dream that it held the answer to my question.

Chapter Two

# Harald's Strange Story

I first heard of Harald Bredesen through Mrs. Norman Vincent Peale, a co-editor, with her husband, of *Guideposts*. We were holding a regular Monday-night editorial meeting when she came in a little out of breath.

"I'm sorry to be late," she said. Then, even before her coat was off, ". . . I've just had dinner with a young man who's given me a real jolt—and a lot to think about."

I had worked with Ruth Peale for ten years. Everyone on the staff valued her for a quality of balance and level-headed good sense. She could always be counted on to bring us back to earth, should our thinking ever become too abstract or wishful. I make a point of this because of the strangeness of the story which Ruth told us that evening. It sounded so fanciful that if it had come from someone else I might have dismissed it rather quickly.

"Have you ever heard the expression, 'speaking in tongues'?" she asked.

Most of us had a vague recollection of the phrase. It came from the Bible, I thought.

" 'Though I speak with the tongues of men and of angels. . . .' That one?" I said.

"That's one reference," Ruth said. "It's mentioned in the Gospels and Paul speaks of it several times, but most of the references are in the book of Acts. Apparently speaking in tongues was a big part of the life of the early Church. Far more than I'd realized.

"Well, my dinner guest said that he had had this experience himself. Not only he, but some of his friends too. Norman and I sat spell-bound for two hours while he told us about people all over the country who are having this happen to them. Apparently, the 'tongue' sometimes turns out to be a real language, which someone listening will understand, although the speaker has never learned it and has no idea what he is saying. It sounds crazy, doesn't it? But there's something about this man. . . ." She paused. "Well, I for one want to know more about it."

After the meeting I told Ruth that I would like to meet her speaker-in-tongues. I thought it might make a good story for the magazine. I did meet him. But the deeper I got into the subject, the more I realized that I had stumbled onto something too big for a single magazine article.

Harald Bredesen is an ordained minister, pastor of the First Reformed Church, Mount Vernon, New York. He is about my age, then in his late thirties. He had a clerical collar, a bald spot and an excitement that was contagious. Bredesen and I had lunch together in a restaurant near my office, and there, in a setting of coffee cups and sugar shakers, he told me a story that seemed to come from a different world.

A few years earlier, Harald Bredesen, although he'd been busily involved in the work of his church, had also been a dissatisfied young man. It seemed to him that his religious life had no vitality to it, especially when he compared his experiences with those of the earliest Christians.

"There was an excitement, a stirring of life in the young

Church," Bredesen said. "The Church today, by and large, has lost this. You've felt it I'm sure. Where are the changed lives? Where are the healings? Where is the belief that men will die for?"

At home in the evenings Bredesen had begun to read the Biblical accounts of the early churches with these questions in mind and almost instantly he fell upon a clue. The more he read, the more he became convinced that first-century Christians received their vitality from the Holy Spirit, and more especially from an experience called, in the New Testament, the Baptism in the Holy Spirit.

Bredesen determined that he was going to have this experience for himself, and he went about it by taking a vacation. He headed for the Allegheny Mountains, ensconced himself in a mountain cabin and there began to pray around the clock. He made up his mind to stay in that cabin until he reached a new level of communication with God. Day after day he kept up his prayer vigil.

At last one morning while he was standing outside the cabin praying aloud, a stillness seemed to settle over the hills. Every fiber of Bredesen's body tensed, as if his whole being were entering into a new plane of awareness. He stopped speaking for a moment. And when he began again, out of his mouth came, and here are his words as I wrote them down that day:

". . . the most beautiful outpouring of vowels and consonants and also some strange, guttural syllables. I could not recognize any of it. It was as though I was listening to a foreign language, except that it was coming out of my own mouth."

Amazed, curious, and a bit frightened, Bredesen ran down the mountain, still talking aloud in this tongue. He came to the edge of a small community. On the stoop of a cabin sat an old man. Bredesen continued to speak in the tongue which was coming so easily and naturally from his lips. The man answered, talking rapidly in a language which Bredesen did not know. When it became obvious that they were not communicating, the old man spoke in English.

"How can you speak Polish but not understand it?" the man asked.

"*I* was speaking in Polish?"

The man laughed, thinking that Bredesen was joking. "Of course it was Polish," he said.

But Bredesen wasn't joking. As far as he could recall he had never before heard the language.

I was still drumming the table-top over that one, when he told me of a second experience, this one in a lobby of a New York hotel. Bredesen was attending a breakfast meeting, and had left his hat on a chair outside the dining room. When time came to leave, he found the chair occupied not by his hat, but by a pretty young lady.

At the time, Bredesen was a bachelor and his male instincts prompted him to extend the conversation beyond a formal excuse-me-have-you-seen-my-hat? The girl noted the clerical collar and in a few minutes they were deep in a conversation on religion. After a while the young lady volunteered the information that her own religious life somehow left her dissatisfied. And soon Bredesen was telling her that he too had felt this lack, but that he had found a new dimension in his devotional life through speaking in tongues.

"Through what?" asked the girl.

"Speaking in a language that God gives you," Bredesen said, and went on to tell her a little about his experience. In the girl's eyes he read disbelief and also something like apprehension.

"Can you speak in these tongues any time you want to?" she said, and he thought she edged almost imperceptibly to the far side of her chair.

"They're given us for prayer."

"Well, can you pray in tongues whenever you want to?"

"Yes. Would you like me to pray this way now?"

The girl looked around the lobby, outright alarm in her eyes this time.

"I won't embarrass you," said Bredesen, and with that he bowed his head slightly and after a short silent prayer began speaking words that to him were unintelligible. The sounds were clipped and full of "p's" and "k's." When he finished, he opened his eyes and saw that the girl's face was ashen.

"Why . . . why . . . I understood you. You were praising God. You were speaking a very old form of Arabic."

"How do you know?" asked Bredesen.

Then he learned that the girl was the daughter of an Egyptologist, that she herself spoke several modern Arabic languages and had studied archaic Arabic.

"You pronounced the words perfectly," she said. "Where on earth did you learn old Arabic?"

Harald Bredesen shook his head. "I didn't," he said. "I didn't know there was such a language."

My interview with Harald Bredesen left me more puzzled than enlightened. Surely there was a logical explanation for the tales he'd told me. Otherwise what he was claiming were out-and-out miracles, and this just didn't jibe with anything I knew of the world today.

Bredesen told me that after his experience he discovered there was a whole branch of Christianity whose hallmark was speaking in tongues. These were the Pentecostals, who take their name from Pentecost when speaking in tongues first occurred. I'd heard of them before, but had never paid much attention; I thought of them as just another of the sects that fringe Christianity.

But what a fringe! In the library I learned that there are 8,500,000 Pentecostals throughout the world, more than 2,000,000 of them in the United States. There were 350 Pentecostal churches and missions in New York City alone, most of them little storefront assemblies in the poorer sections of town.

"It's a curious thing, isn't it," I said to Tib that night at the dinner table, "that I could work on an interfaith magazine all these years, and never step inside a Pentecostal church."

We set out to change that situation. Bredesen had told me that the Rock Church, a Pentecostal congregation in the East Sixties, had a service every Tuesday afternoon. The following Tuesday, Tib made arrangements for a baby sitter and met me in town.

It was very cold when we got out of the taxi at the corner of 62nd Street and Third Avenue. The area is interesting: it used to be one of New York's poor neighborhoods until the elevated train on Third Avenue came down. Now it was in a state of transition, rapidly becoming one of the chic parts of town. The old secondhand furniture stores on the Avenue now sold "antiques," and a dusty hardware store on the corner had become a Brass and Cast Iron Shoppe. A derelict old man was pushing a baby carriage filled with rags and bottles down the sidewalk. Around him stepped a lady walking three poodles; and the poodles wore overcoats.

The church itself was in a white brick building which had once been a private home. The interior was freshly painted in pastel blue, very plain. Behind a choir loft, exhaust fans tried valiantly to keep the air fresh. It was no different from a dozen little churches I'd stepped into, except for one thing: it was so crowded we had trouble finding a place to sit.

"I've never seen anything like this on a Tuesday afternoon," whispered Tib.

We found two seats far at the back, and began to look around. The congregation came from a wider cross-section of society than is true of many churches. There were a few mink coats, there were also blue denim work shirts. I noted several uniforms in the pews: some were nurses from a nearby hospital, some looked like nursemaids who an hour earlier had perhaps been pushing high-wheeled baby carriages in the Park. There was one chauffeur in livery. Perhaps one in five, there that afternoon, was a Negro.

I couldn't tell whether a service was actually in progress or not. The congregation seemed expectant, intent, and yet there didn't seem to be a leader or any set order of worship. A woman in the row ahead of us suddenly spoke aloud. "Blessed Jesus!" she crooned in a voice that was almost singing, and from all over the church came little sighs of agreement. The Negro woman beside us had been sitting with her head raised, eyes tight shut. Now her hands slowly lifted until they were stretched above her head, palms upward, as though she were receiving some ineffable blessing from the air. Now all over the church, arms were raised, hands were opened, in this same gesture of receiving. From the other side of the room a man's voice rang out:

"Praise the Lord!"

The crowd psychology aspect of it fascinated me. I'd heard of a "group mind" but never until we walked into that room did I know that such a thing existed. There was an indefinable bond, an almost palpable concord between the separate human beings in that room. The order was a living, organic thing, not a response to rules or the direction of a chairman, but to some inner urging, like the cells of a body working together.

Every now and then one of the congregation would rise from his seat, walk down the aisle and disappear into a second room in back of the pulpit. After a while the free and easy mood filtered through to me and I leaned over and asked Tib if she wanted to go with me, forward and through the door.

"Let's do," she said.

We entered a room about fifteen feet square, carpeted with a brown rug. Around three walls were straight-backed wooden chairs. There was no other furniture.

Ten or twelve of the chairs were in use, but not for sitting on. Each chair was, in effect, a private altar, with the worshipper kneeling before it, using the seat to rest his arms on. So as not to stand gawking, we knelt too. It was an unnecessary gesture: the people in the room were completely oblivious to our presence. They were praying aloud in low voices and occasionally I caught the word, "Jesus." But as I listened more closely, I perceived that most of the group was not praying in English. Strange sound-combinations and unfamiliar rhythms pulsed around us. They seemed to be praying individually, yet there was a total effect as of group worship. The hum of prayer would swell, then recede.

"This must be praying in tongues," I whispered to Tib.

We stayed in the small room perhaps fifteen minutes. At the end of five the hard floor through the thin carpet was hurting my knees. But the others prayed on, indifferent to comfort.

And then all at once, as if on cue, the voices stopped.

I looked up. No one had entered the room. There was no visible stimulus to have affected everyone the same way, but as a man the group had stopped praying. An elderly woman got slowly to her feet and left the room without speaking to anyone else. A man rose too and left. One by one the people in the little prayer room filed out into the sanctuary. We got up too and returned to our seats, glad that we had left a hymnal to save our places.

Now a tall, angular lady stepped behind the lectern and called out a hymn number. And what singing it was! That whole room exploded into song. The rather stout man on our left sang as if the church's whole reputation depended on him alone. He sang bass, not the bass notes that were written in the book, perhaps, but notes that harmonized well enough with those set down by the composer. And the woman to our right was absolutely transported. Eyes still closed, she sang and swayed, oblivious to everything but the music.

This part I liked, even in spite of the emotionalism. When we got to "Blessed Assurance" (I say "we," because by now Tib and I were singing as loudly as anyone) something happened which I had never seen before. The song leader let the chorus ride. We sang it over and over again: "This is my story, this is my song: Praising my Saviour all the day long." The repetition, instead of being monotonous, had an effect of mounting excitement, an almost intoxicating quality.

And now the clapping started, in the middle of a song. It wasn't a simple beat, but a complex rhythm that was now in double-time, now in half-time, faintly syncopated, weaving in and around the music. This was too great a departure from habit and we didn't join in, but I noticed that the toe of Tib's right shoe was behaving as Pentecostally as anyone's.

The singing didn't cease all at once, but drifted off gradually, and suddenly somewhere down front a man was speaking very loudly in a language I didn't understand. Generations of another tradition in me shuddered at the football-stadium pitch of the voice in a church sanctuary. But no one else seemed to mind. A hush fell over the room. When the man finished, the silence continued. The room was poised, as if waiting for something further. And then, from another quarter, came a second voice. The man was speaking in English, but with the same high-pitched, ecstatic, rapid tones that the speaker in tongues had used. It was an exhortation to ". . . expect great things in these days."

"The Lord has moved mightily," the voice cried. "He has given His promise and He will be faithful in the latter day . . ." and more in the same vein.

I leaned over and asked my neighbor what was happening.

"He's interpreting," the man said. When I became better

versed in the theology of Pentecostalism, I discovered that the "gift of interpretation" is considered on a par with the "gift of tongues," and indeed is thought of as the companion gift which must be sought along with tongues. An "interpretation" purports to give the content of the message just delivered in an unknown tongue, differing from a translation in that the interpreter no more understands the tongue than the speaker does. The interpreter feels that he is mysteriously given a knowledge of what has been said in tongues, and he rises to share this with the congregation. That afternoon, as I say, I grasped nothing of all this. I only noticed that whenever someone spoke loudly enough in tongues for the whole room to hear (and this happened three different times), someone else right away got up and spoke to the room in English.

The sermon on this particular afternoon lasted forty minutes. The text was Moses crossing the Red Sea. An ordinary enough sermon, except for one thing: the preacher depended on the congregation for more support than I was accustomed to. His remarks were punctuated with approving comments from the listeners: "Yes, brother!" and "Amen!" and even "Hallelujah!" which I had never heard voiced outside of Easter music. When he came to a thought that the congregation responded to, he warmed up and let the point ride in something of the same manner that the song leader had let the chorus continue in the hymn singing. "He crossed the sea. Yes, Moses crossed the sea. The waters parted and he crossed over. Moses crossed over the sea!"

The sermon was over. Street lights shined through the front door as the congregation filed down the aisles and out onto the sidewalk. As I struggled into my overcoat I realized that we had been in church on a Tuesday afternoon for the better part of three hours. It was night outside; the well-groomed poodles were being hurried home to supper.

As we headed for our own, we found ourselves in conflict

about the afternoon we had just spent. The time had certainly gone swiftly: for sheer color and action it was like visiting a foreign land at fiesta time. But there was also a deeper excitement to it. I felt intimations of great things there; I also felt embarrassment that people should exhibit emotions in front of others, and just plain puzzlement in the face of unfamiliar forms.

On the way out of the little church, I had asked the preacher where their particular form of worship came from.

"Why, from the Bible," he said. "The last part of First Corinthians, Chapter 14."

That night, by the fire in our living room in Chappaqua, Tib and I looked it up. There, as if they had been written about the service that afternoon, were the words of Paul:

What then, brethren? When you come together, each one has a hymn, a lesson, a revelation, a tongue, or an interpretation. Let all things be done for edification. If any speak in a tongue, let there be only two or at most three, and each in turn; and let one interpret. But if there is no one to interpret, let each of them keep silent in church and speak to himself and to God.... So, my brethren, earnestly desire to prophesy, and do not forbid speaking in tongues; but all things should be done decently and in order.[1]

That night after Tib had gone upstairs, I sat alone for a while, the room lit only by an occasional flame from the dying fire. And it occurred to me that the fire was a little like the experience I had gone through with Christ. That relationship had blazed brightly for a while and was now burning low.

Would it use up the fuel of a single experience and grow cold? I had been reading the book of Acts, and it was clear to me that the Christians in the early Church had not grown cold in their experience of Christ. Nor had these Pentecostals, worshipping in their funny little church on a Tuesday afternoon. For all the strangeness of their service, it seemed to me that these people were experiencing a present company with Christ that I could understand because I had had it too, once: in the hospital. Maybe their language was strange, and their actions peculiar; but if you looked behind that, if you looked into their faces instead of at their mannerisms, you saw joy and you saw life.

Chapter Three

# Surprise Witness

It was snowing, blowing, and very cold the next morning. About ten o'clock the boys and I went out to dig a path through the drifts for the mailman. Somehow, the intoxication of yesterday seemed very far away. Between shovelfuls I told Scott and Donn about the service we had attended. But at nine years old and six years old, their chief reaction was amazement that anyone would go to church when it wasn't even Sunday.

I had some outgoing letters to give to the mailman, so I posted three-year-old Elizabeth at a downstairs window to watch for him, and went back upstairs to my office in the attic. The boys' school was closed on account of the snow, and as I listened to the ebb and flow of fortunes in the Monopoly game downstairs, it swept over me suddenly that the kids were right. That church service yesterday had been pretty silly. It was rude to jump up in the middle of a church service and talk out loud. It was ridiculous to wave your hands about over your head. I had been right in the first place: it was all an interesting study in group psychology.

"He's coming!" in tones of great excitement Elizabeth announced the mailman. I went down and exchanged letters with him.

The first one he handed me had a Mount Vernon postmark, and I knew it would be from Harald Bredesen. I was disenchanted with the whole subject of far-out phenomena; back upstairs I found myself moving Harald's letter to the bottom of the pile. At last it lay on the desk alone and I opened it without enthusiasm. Inside were several pages torn from *Life* magazine, with a little note scribbled across the top one: "Thought you'd be interested in this. H.B."

I was interested, partly because it was written by a man I knew: Dr. Henry Pitney Van Dusen, then the president of Union Theological Seminary in New York. But I was especially interested when I saw the subject. Dr. Van Dusen was writing about what he called the "Third Force" in Christianity, and he dealt in part with the Pentecostals.

What would the president of one of the great intellectual centers of the country have to say about these most non-intellectual people? I poured the last of the breakfast coffee from the pot and settled down to read about the trip that Dr. Van Dusen had just completed around the world. He stopped in twenty countries and in each he visited top leaders of the traditional Protestant churches. Everywhere he met with the same deep concern over the phenomenal growth of the "nonconformist" religious bodies, especially the Pentecostals.

"Are you worried," he asked an Anglican bishop, "because these new movements are reaching people you have not reached, or because they are drawing off your own adherents?"

"Both," was the reply.

By the time Dr. Van Dusen had finished digesting the information he had gathered on his trip, he was speaking of ". . . a third, mighty arm of Christendom," standing boldly alongside the Catholic and Protestant arms. And at the hard center core of this third force was the Pentecostal revival.

There are several sources of strength which have made the third force the most extraordinary religious phenomenon of our time [wrote Dr. Van Dusen]. Its groups preach a direct Biblical message readily understood. They commonly promise an immediate life-transforming experience of the living-God-in-Christ which is far more significant to many individuals than the version of it found in conventional churches.

They directly approach people—in their homes, or on the streets, anywhere—and do not wait for them to come to church. They have great spiritual ardor, which is sometimes but by no means always excessively emotional. They shepherd their converts in an intimate, sustaining group-fellowship: a feature of every vital Christian renewal since the Holy Spirit descended on the disciples at the first Pentecost. They place strong emphasis on the Holy Spirit—so neglected by many traditional Christians—as the immediate, potent presence of God both in each human soul and in the Christian fellowship. Above all they expect their followers to practice an active, untiring, seven-days-a-week Christianity.

Until lately, other Protestants regarded the movement as a temporary and passing phenomenon, not worth much attention. Now there is a growing, serious recognition of its true dimensions, and probable permanence. The tendency to dismiss its Christian message as inadequate is being replaced by a chastened readiness to investigate the secrets of its mighty sweep.[1]

It was a remarkable statement.

I wanted to know more, so I wrote Dr. Van Dusen that same afternoon, asking for an interview.

Some ten days later Tib and I went together to see him. The visit was particularly meaningful to me because my own father had taught at Union until his death. Sitting in the Van Dusens' apartment at the seminary, I could look across the quadrangle to the office which my father had occupied. Just around the corner, I knew, was my parents' old apartment, where for six years we had brought the children each Sunday for a visit. The return, now, was full of memories.

Dr. Van Dusen must have sensed what this homecoming meant to Tib and me, because he had gone to no little trouble to prepare tea. Trouble, because both his wife and his housekeeper were out, and he had made the tea himself. He sat down opposite us, now, and tasted the brew.

"Too strong," he said, shaking his head. "Too strong. I've brought some ginger ale—maybe we can cut it with a bit of this."

He took another taste of the concoction of too-strong tea and ginger ale, made a face, and put it down. "Have some cookies," he said. "I'm really glad to see you. You know, perhaps, that I'm very much interested in the Pentecostals."

Dr. Van Dusen told us about the trip to the Caribbean, some years earlier, when he had attended a Pentecostal service for the first time. "You know," he said, "that was a terrible indictment. To think that the president of Union should have to travel all the way to the Caribbean to attend his first Pentecostal service. Shocking."

Dr. Van Dusen had come away from this experience with several impressions. The first was a strange one.

"I felt rather at home," he said. "In spite of the vast differences—and they were certainly vast—I felt at home. I felt that I was stepping back in time to a primitive but very vital Christian experience. I do believe that Peter and Barnabas and Paul would find themselves more at home in a good Pentecostal service than in the formalized and ritualized worship of most of our modern churches."

He came away, too, with an impression about tongues. As we had, he had watched and listened, fascinated, to people praying "in the Spirit."

"It seemed to me," he said, "that this speaking in tongues was a kind of spiritual therapy. It was quite unsettling, hearing tongues for the first time. But one impression stands out above the rest. I came away feeling that this was an emotional release of an ultimately healthy kind. It left people better off: released, relaxed.

"I've never had this experience," Dr. Van Dusen continued, "but I can understand it best when I think of some of our great poets. They quite often reach a point where they simply are not communicating intelligible ideas. Blake, for instance, and Auden, and Gerard Manley Hopkins. All of them have written completely irrational phrases. They 'don't make sense.' This, it seems to me, is what the irrational nature of tongues is all about. The human heart finally reaches a point where words—the dictionary definition of words—simply aren't adequate to express all that cries out to be said."

I was amazed at the seriousness he was placing on all this. But it was just before we left that Dr. Van Dusen made the statement which tilted the scale for me, which made me decide definitely that I wanted to find out all I could about the Pentecostals.

It was time to leave. Tib was on her feet, but Dr. Van Dusen remained seated; clearly he had one more thing to say.

"I have come to feel," he said, choosing his words carefully, "that the Pentecostal movement with its emphasis upon the Holy Spirit, is more than just another revival. It is a revolution in our day. It is a revolution comparable in importance with the establishment of the original Apostolic Church and with the Protestant Reformation."

It took me a while to grasp the significance of these words. Dr. Van Dusen was saying that this revival—yes, as represented in part by the arm-waving, tongues-speaking, hand-clapping little church Tib and I had visited on a Tuesday afternoon—was not to be compared with some crazy, backwash sect. It was not to be compared even with the founding of a major Protestant denomination such as Presbyterianism or Methodism; it was comparable instead to Protestantism and Catholicism themselves.

Tib and I drove home with heads reeling. How was it possible for Dr. Van Dusen to compare Pentecostalism with the founding of the original Church! Was he all by himself in this feeling? Over the next few weeks I read widely on the subject. And just in this skimming over the surface I discovered two vital clues.

First I learned that the Pentecostal movement was far more widespread than I had dreamed. It included not only the 8,000,000 members of "Pentecostal churches"; more significantly, it included an unguessable number of people in the traditional established churches, both Catholic and Protestant, who were experiencing the very same manifestations of a supernatural and unexplainable power in their midst.

And second I discovered that Dr. Van Dusen was by no means alone in his evaluation of this phenomemon. Key figures in both the Protestant and the Catholic churches were expressing parallel concern. I made a list and tucked it away in a file I had started under the label "Tongues Stories" and promised myself that someday I would see these men.

The trouble was that these researches were threatening to take more time than I could spare. The subject fascinated me, but meanwhile there were the magazine assignments that produced our income. I felt an increasing frustration over it because I sensed that I had stumbled onto that Big Story that comes to every writer just once. And I couldn't do anything about it.

And then something happened which completely changed the situation. At a neighborhood dinner party one night, I told the story of Harald Bredesen's speaking Polish. I'd found it sure dinner-party fare: no matter what outbursts of indignation or hilarity it inspired, it always seemed to interest people. But that night there was a man at the party I had never met before, Sam Peters. As we got up from the table, Peters drew me aside.

"You know," he said, "I'm fascinated with this story. I'd like to hear more. Could you come to my office?"

Peters, it turned out, worked for a book publishing house. I did go to visit him in his office in Manhattan and several weeks later found myself contracting for a book on the whole phenomenon of tongues and what they might mean, the publisher to support the research.

"There's one thing we'd better keep straight," I said to Peters at the end of our conversation. "You keep saying, 'these tongues of yours.' They're not my tongues, Peters, and won't be either. I'm interested, I'm intrigued, but I'm certainly not buying. I'm an Episcopalian, you know, and I guess we're a pretty stuffy lot."

Peters smiled. "I know. No one's asking you to get involved. Just do a good job reporting. That's all we ask."

"Good," I said. "Then we understand each other. I've always said the best reporter, anyway, is the one who keeps his distance."

Chapter Four

# Stone's Folly

Distance from these people, I began to feel, was going to be a very simple quantity to maintain.

I was sitting in the main reading room of the New York Public Library, a pile of out-of-print books on the desk in front of me, and the world into which they were taking me seemed about as far removed from my own suburbia as anything could be. I was trying to track down the very first instance of someone's speaking in tongues in modern times. One early candidate was a mountaineer farmer. One was an itinerant colored preacher. One, a man who ran a school that charged no tuition. There were Indians in Chile, African natives, outcasts in India. Tib summed up the gulf that divided us.

"Not a one of them," she said when I reported the results of my research, "ever worried about chinchbugs in the lawn."

She was right. Not many had had lawns to worry about, and the one who did put a cow on it to graze:

It was in the United States in the year 1900 that a young Methodist minister, Charles F. Parham, decided he must do something about his religious life. He had been reading the book of Acts and the letters of Paul and comparing the feebleness he found in his own ministry with the power reflected there. Where were his new converts? Where were his miracles? His healings? Surely, he said to himself, the Christians of the first century had a secret which he and his church no longer possessed.

In October, 1900, Parham set out to try to find that secret.

He had concluded that it would require a more thorough study of the Bible than he could achieve by himself. So he decided to open a Bible school, where he would be both director and one of the students. He would charge no tuition, each student simply supplying what he could toward expenses.

The first matter on the agenda was locating a suitable building at a rent of little—or nothing—a month. And Parham did find such a building in Topeka, Kansas. It was not only large, but picturesque. A Topeka citizen named Stone had started to build a mansion for himself. Halfway through, he ran out of money. The downstairs was magnificent: carved staircases, massive fireplaces, expensive paneling. But the upstairs was finished in the cheapest pine. Around Topeka, the building had a nickname. It was called "Stone's Folly."

Charles Parham moved into Stone's Folly, and announced that anyone who wanted to join him there in a study of the New Testament was welcome. Forty students showed up. They must have given Topeka more to talk about than Stone himself had done. They came in buggies and wagons and on foot, bringing with them their wives and children. They brought what they needed to keep house, and soon Stone's magnificent mansion had diapers hanging from a line in the back yard and a cow grazing on the lawn in front.

Charles Parham knew the direction that their studies should take. For fifty years many Protestants had been paying increasing attention to a religious experience that occurs, traditionally, some time *after* conversion. It was a day-and-date-able experience which some people called "a second work of grace," some "the second blessing," some "sanctification." But the essence of the experience was always an encounter with the Holy Spirit.

The promise of some kind of new relationship with the Holy Spirit weaves like a thread through the New Testament. From the very opening chapters of the Gospels it is forecast. The Jews, for a while, thought that John the Baptist might be the promised Messiah. But John told them, "There cometh one mightier than I after me, the lachet of whose shoes I am not worthy to stoop down and unloose. I indeed," he said, "have baptized you with water; but he shall baptize you with the Holy Ghost." [1] The Baptism with the Holy Spirit, John was saying, would be the distinguishing mark of the Messiah.

Toward the last of His life, Christ began to put increasing emphasis on the Holy Spirit. He would be the comforter of the disciples, standing by them in trouble, leading them into truth, taking His place when He was gone. After His crucifixion Christ appeared to His disciples and told them that they must stay in Jerusalem.

"You must wait," He said, "for the promise made by my Father, about which you have heard me speak: John, as you know, baptized with water, but you will be baptized with the Holy Spirit, and within the next few days." [2]

The disciples did wait as they were instructed. And then:

While the day of Pentecost was running its course they were all together in one place, when suddenly there came from the sky a noise like that of a strong driving wind, which filled the whole house where they were sitting. And there appeared to them tongues like flames of fire, dispersed among them and resting on each one. And they were all filled with the Holy Spirit, and began to talk in other tongues, as the Spirit gave them power of utterance. [3]

From this infilling with the Holy Spirit the Church dates its beginning. It was new, small, surrounded with enemies, and yet this young Church had power: to heal, to convince, to spread. The churches which evolved with the passing of time kept in their traditions a vestige of this early dependence on a specific filling with the Holy Spirit as the source of their power. Roman Catholics, Lutherans, Episcopalians all preserve, in their Confirmation services, the idea that it is at this moment that the confirmee receives a special gift of power to be an effective Christian.

But groups like the Wesleyan Methodists and the Holiness people glimpsed the fact that this ceremony of Confirmation was often just a ritual, often failed really to impart power. They stressed the Baptism as an experience that did not come automatically but which had to be sought over and over, if necessary, until the Christian was certain he had been filled with the Holy Spirit.

But how could a person be certain? Some said there was no direct evidence, that you accepted, by faith, the fact that you had been so baptized. Others said that you knew you had received the Holy Spirit when your prayer life became filled with power. But this was a somewhat indefinite criterion. The task which Charles Parham and his fellow Bible students set themselves was to uncover a criterion which could be counted on.

At Stone's Folly, Parham and his friends spent their time reading the Bible, washing dishes, milking the cow, praying, seeking such a sure evidence of the presence of the Holy Spirit.

In December Parham had to go away on a three-day trip. Before he left Topeka he gave his students an assignment.

"While I'm gone," he said, "I want you to read the book of Acts. Study every account where the Baptism is received for the first time. See if you can find any constant factor, any common denominator."

On his return he found the school humming with excitement. The students, studying independently, had all come to the same conclusion. In the five different descriptions in Acts of the Baptism being received for the first time, it seemed to them that the curious phenomenon called "speaking in tongues" was either definitely stated as occurring or could be deduced from what the account did record.

The first time was at Pentecost. "And they were all filled with the Holy Ghost, and began to speak with other tongues, as the spirit gave them utterance." [4]

The second was in Samaria.

Now when the apostles which were at Jerusalem heard that Samaria had received the word of God, they sent unto them Peter and John: who, when they were come down, prayed for them, that they might receive the Holy Ghost (for as yet he was fallen upon none of them: only they were baptized in the name of the Lord Jesus).

Then laid they their hands on them, and they received the Holy Ghost. And when Simon saw that through laying on of the apostles' hands the Holy Ghost was given, he offered them money, saying, Give me also this power that on whomsoever I lay hands, he may receive the Holy Ghost. [5]

The third time was at Damascus, when Paul received the Baptism.

And Ananias went his way, and entered into the house; and putting his hands on him said, Brother Saul, the Lord, even Jesus, that appeared unto thee in the way as thou camest, hath sent me, that thou mightest receive thy sight, and be filled with the Holy Ghost. And immediately there fell from his eyes as if it had been scales: and he received sight forthwith, and arose, and was baptized. [6]

The fourth time was at Caesarea, when the household of Cornelius received the Baptism. "While Peter yet spake these words, the Holy Ghost fell on them which heard the word. And they of the circumcision which believed were astonished, as many as came with Peter, because that on the Gentiles also was poured out the gift of the Holy Ghost. For they heard them speak with tongues . . ." [7]

And the fifth recorded instance occurred at Ephesus.

And it came to pass, that, while Apollos was at Corinth, Paul having passed through the upper coasts came to Ephesus: and finding certain disciples, he said unto them, Have ye received the Holy Ghost since ye believed? And they said unto him, We have not so much as heard whether there be any Holy Ghost. . . .And when Paul had laid his hands upon them, the Holy Ghost came on them; and they spake with tongues, and prophesied.[8]

Parham was intrigued but not convinced. "I see tongues in three of the Baptisms," he said, "but not at Samaria. Nor in Paul's case."

"No," said his students, "but we know that Paul did have the gift of tongues later in his ministry. 'I thank my God, I speak with tongues more than ye all,' he told the Corinthians.[9] When did he receive this gift? Could it have been at his Baptism?"

Parham considered this in silence. "What about Samaria?" he said at last.

"At Samaria, Simon the Magician was so impressed by something he saw when people were filled with the Holy Ghost that he offered money to get this power for himself. What could he have seen that was so special? Not miracles, or healings, because he'd already seen Christians doing these things. He'd been following Philip around for weeks just because of such signs. No, when Peter and John arrived and Samarian Christians received the Holy Ghost, Simon saw something new, something different. Might it have been tongues?"

The excitement infected Parham too. Could this really be the evidence they had been looking for? It was late at night. "I wonder what would happen," he said, "if tomorrow we were all of us together to pray to receive the Baptism in the same way it is described in the Bible: with speaking in tongues?"

The next morning, everyone in Stone's Folly joined in this prayer. They prayed throughout the morning and into the afternoon. The atmosphere around the mansion was charged with expectancy. But the sun went down and still nothing unusual had occurred.

Then, at about seven o'clock that night—it was New Year's Eve, 1900—a young student named Agnes N. Ozman remembered something. Wasn't it true that many of the Baptisms described in Acts were accompanied by an action, as well as prayer: didn't the person offering the prayer often put his hands on the one who wished to receive the Baptism? In the Bible she found the reference she remembered. There it was; at Samaria, at Damascus, at Ephesus, always the word "hands." "Putting his hands on him. . . ." "Then laid they their hands on them. . . ."

Miss Ozman went to find Charles Parham. She told him about her new thought.

"Would you pray for me in this way?" she asked.

Parham hesitated just long enough to utter a short prayer about the rightness of what they were doing. Then, gently, he placed his two hands on Miss Ozman's head. Immediately, quietly, there came from her lips a flow of syllables which neither one of them could understand.

The Pentecostals look back on this hour—7:00 P.M., New Year's Eve, 1900—as one of the key dates in their history. They point to it as the first time since the days of the early Church that the Baptism in the Holy Spirit had been sought, where speaking in tongues was expected as the initial evidence.

At Stone's Folly, everyone now prayed with increased fervor for the coming of the Holy Spirit. One of the large unfinished rooms on the top floor of the mansion was turned into a prayer room in a conscious effort to recreate the setting of the Upper Room in Jerusalem at Pentecost. Over the next three days there were many Baptisms, each one signaled by the mysterious tongues. On January 3, Parham himself and a dozen other ministers from various denominations present with him in this room received the Baptism, and spoke with tongues. In their excitement they made plans for a grand missionary tour which would carry the new message from Topeka across the country and into Canada.

They got exactly as far as Kansas City.

There they were met with open hostility. No one would listen to the message Parham was so sure of. He and his fellow ministers were pulled apart by the local clergy and newspapers. The little group broke up. Parham was without supporters and without funds. He was without a pulpit. At last he was even without food. Within a few weeks Parham was back in Topeka, and there he received another blow. Stone's Folly was to be sold. The old monstrosity that had meant so much to the little school had to be abandoned, and with the loss of their meeting place, the school itself disbanded.

Charles Parham began preaching on street corners. He called his ministry a "full Gospel" message: meaning that he believed the Gospel should be preached in its entirety, not leaving out tongues, or healing, or any of the other gifts promised through the Spirit. Three years passed, and still no one listened. And then, in the summer of 1903, Parham arrived in the health resort town of El Dorado Springs, Missouri. And it was here that a dramatic change in his ministry occurred.

The waters at El Dorado were said to be good for all sorts of aches and pains, and Parham took advantage of the atmosphere of need by preaching on the very steps of the springs. After each sermon he invited anyone who was sick or in pain to come for further prayers to the tiny cottage he and his wife had rented nearby. Many came. And from the first many reported their condition improved. Word got around that here

was a man gifted with unusual powers. And it was clear that
he was not out for personal gain: he never charged a fee, never
took up a collection.

One of the people to come to his free healing services was a
woman named Mary Arthur. Mrs. Arthur was losing her sight.
She had already had two operations, and with each her condition worsened. On the day she visited the Parhams' cottage,
she could only see out of one eye, and then only with pain.

During the service, Parham laid his hands on her eyes and
prayed that the Spirit would flow through him, to heal. Mrs.
Arthur rose from her knees shaken and unbelieving. Whereas
only minutes before she had had to keep her eyes closed to
avoid pain, now she could look directly toward the light without the slightest discomfort.

Mrs. Arthur returned to her home in Galena, Kansas, and
began telling everyone about this wonderful new ministry. A
few weeks later she invited the Parhams to come to Galena,
and to hold services in her home. Their decision to accept her
invitation marked the turning point in their career, because in
Galena the Pentecostal message caught fire.

In just a few days' time, the living room of the Arthurs'
house was crowded to overflowing. Friends erected a tent on
the vacant lot next door. This too was outgrown almost immediately, as people poured into Galena from miles around.
Parham and his friends leased an old warehouse on the edge
of town. Winter was coming on: for warmth they set potbel-
lied stoves around the sides of the large room; pews were
improvised by laying planks across barrels. And there in the
warehouse-church, Charles Parham preached Christ's ministry
complete with the Baptism in the Holy Spirit.

Night after night people swarmed into the rough church, to
leave hours later with stories of healings and strange mystic
experiences. The Cincinnati *Inquirer* sent a man to Galena to
cover the revival.

It is doubtful [wrote the correspondent], whether in recent years anything has occurred that has awakened the interest, excited the comment, or mystified the people of this region as have the religious meetings being held here by Rev. C. F. Parham....

Almost three months have elapsed since this man came to Galena, and during that time he has healed over a thousand people and converted more than 800.... People who have not walked for years without the aid of crutches have risen from the altar with their limbs so straightened that they were able to lay aside their crutches.... Here the followers receive what they term "the Pentecost" and are enabled to speak in foreign tongues, languages with which they are, when free from this power, utterly unfamiliar. This alone is considered one of the most remarkable things of the meeting. Last week a woman arose during the meeting and spoke for ten minutes, no one apparently in the audience knowing what she said. An Indian, who had come from the Pawnee Reservation in the territory that day to attend the services, stated that she was speaking in the language of his tribe, and that he could understand every word of the testimony....[10]

Parham stayed in Galena over three months, teaching, preaching and healing. When he finally left, it was to fullfill a dream that had been with him since the closing of Stone's Folly: he wanted to start another school. Five years, almost to the day, after he opened his school in Topeka, he announced the founding of a second, this time in Houston, Texas.

It was to this school that a student came who was destined to become another key figure in the story of the Pentecostals: W. J. Seymour, an ordained Negro minister. It was Seymour who carried the Pentecostal message to California, to one of the most famous addresses in Pentecostal history: 312 Azusa Street, Los Angeles.

Seymour arrived in Los Angeles, suitcase in hand, never guessing the furor he was to touch off. He had been invited to preach in a small Negro church there. Fresh from his experi-

ence in Parham's school, Seymour opened what was intended
to be a series of sermons with an address on the Holy Spirit
and the phenomenon of speaking in tongues. That was too
much for the elders of the little church. The next day, when
Seymour arrived to speak, he found the doors of the church
locked.

One of the members of the church, however, did not agree
with this treatment. She told Mr. Seymour that if he wanted
to, he was welcome to preach in her own home. The house
was on the old side, she admitted, but it was better than
nothing.

For three days Seymour preached there, quietly and logically presenting the Biblical background to his position. But
on the evening of April 9, 1906, as he was speaking, people
listening began to receive the Baptism. They spoke in
tongues, they laughed, they shouted and sang until the scene
must have paralleled the original Pentecost, when Peter and
his companions were accused of being drunk with new wine.

The news spread. By early the next morning, a large crowd
was packed into the rickety old house, and many more were
outside waiting for a chance to get in. The shouting and singing, the "Hallelujahs" and "Praise the Lords" resounded
from the rafters. Hand clapping and feet stomping began: the
old building began to shake. No one noticed. Then, with one
particularly loud "Praise the Lord!" the foundations gave
way: the floors collapsed, the walls caved in, the roof fell.

No one was hurt. But it was clear that the rapidly growing
meeting needed larger (and sturdier) quarters. After a bit of
searching they located just the place: 312 Azusa Street.

The Azusa Street address was in an unpretentious part of
town. The neighbors were a lumberyard, a stable and a tomb-
stone factory. But at least no one would be disturbed by the
"new wine" exuberance of the congregation. The two-story
building itself had once been a livery stable, but had been
partially destroyed by fire and was now abandoned. A flat roof

replaced the burned one, giving the structure a sawed-off look. The worshippers whitewashed the outside of the building, dragged nail kegs inside for seats. Seymour himself sat quietly at one end of the big downstairs room praying constantly and preaching rarely. He was the leader, but he led more by suggestion than by direction.

The Azusa Street revival lasted for three years. Rich and poor alike came to see what was going on. People came from nearby towns, from the Middle West, from New England, Canada, Great Britain. There were whites and colored, old and young, educated and illiterate. Reporters from all over the country came to investigate, and whether they filed reports that were favorable or unfavorable, they always had a good story.

During my research I was in correspondence with one of the few surviving eyewitnesses to the Azusa Street revival. He is Mr. Harvey McAlister of Springfield, Missouri, who wrote me that he had visited the mission himself many times. He had one especially interesting incident to relate:

My brother, Robert E. McAlister, now deceased, was in Los Angeles when the following incident took place and he reported it to me. The girl, whom I knew intimately, and I heard the incident also from her parents, was Kathleen Scott.

This ... took place in what is known as Old Azusa Street Mission. People traveled from every part of the world to investigate what was happening there. There was a large auditorium with an "Upper Room," upstairs. The place was open day and night for several years, with preaching services two or three times daily, and people in prayer in the Upper Room day and night. At the close of the preaching crowds would retire to the Upper Room to pray. When time came for preaching, someone would ring a bell and all would come downstairs for the services.

Kathleen was in the Upper Room, teen-age, at this particular time. A man entered the building, the service now being in process, and hearing people pray, he ventured upstairs to the prayer room. The moment he entered, Kathleen, moved by the Spirit, arose and pointed to the man as he stood at the head of the stairway, and spoke in a language other than her own for several minutes.

The ringing of the bell, calling the people to the preaching service, interrupted. All the people arose and made their way to the stairway. The man, as Kathleen approached the stairs, took her arm and directed her downstairs, to the speaker's desk and waited until order was restored in the auditorium. Then he spoke.

"I am a Jew, and I came to this city to investigate this speaking in tongues. No person in this city knows my first or my last name, as I am here under an assumed name. No one in this city knows my occupation, or anything about me. I go to hear preachers for the purpose of taking their sermons apart, and using them in lecturing against the Christian religion.

"This girl, as I entered the room, started speaking in the Hebrew language. She told me my first name and my last name, and she told me why I was in the city and what my occupation was in life, and then she called upon me to repent. She told me things about my life which it would be impossible for any person in this city to know."

Then [Mr. McAlister's letter concludes], the man dropped to his knees and cried and prayed as though his heart would break.

This was the Azusa Street revival. Without fanfare, without advertisements, or choirs, or bands, or any of the usual accompaniments of revival, the movement which was born in an old livery stable swept ahead. All day, all night, for over 1000 days.

Chapter Five

# A Crazy Way to Grow

Spring, 1960, had come, and with it the change of seasonal foliage in our garage. Down from their nails and into storage went the snow shovels, out came the spreader and the mower. A circular appeared in the mailbox: "Will you be PROUD when friends look at your lawn this summer?" and I found myself thinking of the cow on the front lawn at Stone's Folly.

Spring had come, and my journey into the strange world of the Pentecostals was still a safe and remote affair, involving me personally no more than would a trip through a foreign country where I might see men and women at their work through the window of a fast-moving train.

One thing I was ready to grant: something mysterious and out of the ordinary had certainly been at work during those first years of the Pentecostal revival. All around the world Pentecostal churches had sprung up, all roughly at the same time: bracketing within a few years the turn of the century. The odd part about it was that there was often no discernible tie between the different groups, no connection to which a historian could point and say, "Church B developed out of Church A."

Some of the earliest visitors to the Azusa Street mission, for example, were a group of Armenian immigrants who found nothing new in the Pentecostal manifestation. Twenty years before a similar movement, with speaking in tongues, had appeared among the Presbyterians in Armenia. When these Pentecostal Presbyterians immigrated to California they brought their ways of worship with them, and had remained alone and isolated until they discovered to their surprise that a parallel movement was underway at Azusa Street.

In the midst of the Unicois mountains in North Carolina, members of the little Camp Creek Baptist Church began quite independently to speak in tongues: they had had no contact with tongues-speaking people before, in fact had not known that such a phenomenon existed.

In India members of the staid Church Missionary Society of Great Britain were surprised when a sixteen-year-old Indian girl began to speak a language that no one could identify, whenever she prayed. The canon of the cathedral at Bombay was consulted; he invited friends to pray with the girl in the hope of finding someone who would understand the language. At last someone did: the language, he reported, was Arabic, and the prayers she was offering were for the safety of the Church in Libya, a country of which, as far as anyone knew, she had never heard. Now other Indian Christians began to experience this phenomenon of speaking unlearned languages, and soon a full-fledged revival was underway. The story was published in a leaflet put out by the mission in September, 1906. The circular was in print and being distributed when the first news reached India of similar events taking place in the United States!

I was intrigued by these seemingly spontaneous and unrelated outcroppings of tongues in widely separated parts of the world. What did it mean?

Even when the impetus for one experience was clearly traceable to another, the readiness with which the new message was seized upon seemed to me unusual. It was as if the emotional and spiritual soil of the times were such that a single pamphlet appearing among the right people at the right time could spark an entire movement. Miss Minnie Abrams, one of the women at the C.M.S. mission in India, wrote a small booklet about her experiences there which she sent to selected friends throughout the world. One arrived at the manse of the Methodist Episcopal Church in Valparaiso, Chile. The pastor, W. C. Hoover, read it with great interest. This is his description of what happened:

During the year or more which had elapsed since receiving the booklet we had shared with our people the strange, good news. Now . . . we purposed with our whole heart to have a revival. On the very first night . . . on calling for prayer, a most astonishing thing happened—the whole congregation, of perhaps 150, burst forth as one man in audible prayer! Remarkable manifestations and dreams occurred to one and another, and . . . these culminated in experiences with a great number of people that are very adequately described in numerous particulars in Acts 2. Multitudes came to see . . . the attendances grew by leaps and bounds. The Sunday evening attendance exceeded 900.[1]

Sometimes the revival spread to one place simply as the result of a newspaper story about revival someplace else. The movement reached South China in this way. Missionaries at the Wuchow Schools read in the paper about the strange happenings at Azusa Street. One Saturday night a while later, in the middle of a quiet prayer meeting, one of the Wuchow faculty began to speak a language he did not understand. It was the beginning of a large Chinese revival.

The men and women who pioneered the modern Pentecostal movement were in the main quiet, unprepossessing people. There was no Luther among them, no Knox or Calvin, no Fox, no Wesley, no outstanding individual drawing adherents to his message by sheer force of personality. The people who came to Azusa Street were very average sorts, often poor, frequently uneducated. But wherever they returned home, something in what they had to say caught fire. Soon little groups of Pentecostals were springing up where these people lived. In Chicago, in Winnipeg, New York and Little Rock. And further afield: in London and Sunderland, Amsterdam and Oslo, in Calcutta and Allagahad and Mukti— for people had come to Azusa Street from all over the world.

Everywhere the story was the same. Ordinary people returned home with a message and found it instantly received. It seemed to need no selling—fortunately, for they were no salesmen. Often it was as though their hearers had been waiting all along for this news; there was a flash of recognition and the job of persuasion was done.

But alongside this wild-fire, seemingly effortless spread of the Pentecostal message was an opposite reaction, equally strong, equally instantaneous: bitter antagonism.

I could recognize the emotion. I'd felt it myself in a mild form the day after our visit to Rock Church, when I was suddenly repelled by the whole subject and wanted to hear no more about it. But this reaction on my part was the merest summer shower compared with the hurricane of opposition that the Pentecostals brought on in some quarters.

The setting was a one-room, frame schoolhouse at Camp Creek, in the North Carolina mountains. A revival was under way. People came from as far as thirty miles away, on foot or in ox-drawn wagons. During the day, the people gathered on the slope outside the schoolhouse. At night they met indoors by lamplight. At each day's gathering there was a mounting sense of expectancy.

In seasons of fervent prayer [writes Charles W. Conn in his intriguing account of this revival],[2] one or two of the members were so enraptured with the One to whom they prayed that they were curiously exercised by the Holy Spirit . . . they spoke in languages unknown to those who heard the utterances. What had happened, the simple rustic Christians could not understand, for within the memory of the oldest members no such thing had been known. A total ignorance of Church history prevented their knowledge of similar manifestations in other periods of awakening and revival. Soon others began to have similar ecstatic experiences, and regardless of the place, time or circumstances contingent to the experience, one manifestation was uniform in all: they spoke in tongues, or languages unknown to those who listened in wonder and hope. . . .

News of the great spiritual outpouring raced like a prairie fire in every direction until the curious and the believing rushed side by side to witness this strange thing. In distant countries the plowing was stopped at midday; the churning was left to sour in the crocks; the cows were milked while the sun was high; and the oxen were given hasty provender, and the wagons were headed over the hills toward Camp Creek.

At the very first the reception of the revival by local churches was excellent. Men went home to their own communities and told of changed lives and of a new relationship with Christ. The clergymen could hardly believe their ears; they urged their people to attend.

And then the reaction set in. It came as unexpectedly and as swiftly as the original revival. Overnight, church leaders turned hostile. The elders of one Baptist church barred thirty-three members from a conference; their offence: they had spoken in tongues. A group of ministers went to some county officials and persuaded them to withdraw permission to use the school. When the revivalists gathered one night they found doors and windows tightly locked. Undeterred, they simply built a small log church of their own.

The opposition took stronger measures. A group of farmers one rainy night crept up to the new church and set fire to it. The rain put the fire out, so a few nights later they demolished the church with dynamite. The revivalists rebuilt. Then one morning—this time in broad daylight—more than 100 men converged on the little church building. Among them were ordained ministers, deacons, elders, a justice of the peace and a sheriff. While members of the church stood helplessly by, this vigilante group pulled the church apart log by log, piled the timbers by the roadside and set fire to them. By pulling the church apart beforehand, they pointed out, they were not burning hallowed property: they were simply setting fire to a heap of wood.

The revivalists did not try to rebuild a second time, but began to meet instead in each others' homes. So the vigilante committee used more personal tactics. They hauled members of the new congregation from their beds at night and whipped them. Each morning the yards of homes where services had been held were littered with stones and broken glass. Rifles were fired through cabin windows. Streams were polluted, homes burned to the ground. These acts of violence continued for several years, but were finally stilled by the voice of a woman.

Her name was Emiline Allen, and she was the wife of one of the new movement's leaders. One day a group was holding a service in the Allens' home when twenty-five or thirty men trooped into the yard brandishing clubs, knives, and guns and demanding that the congregation disperse or have the house burned down around their heads.

Allen's dauntless wife, Emiline, with sweet and disarming authority [Conn relates], confronted the men in the yard and bade them enter, which they refused to do with muted murmurings and fatuous threatenings. . . . Said she, "There's no reason to hide behind masks when I know every one of you. You're our neighbors, so you have no cause to hide when you visit our home. Now take off that garb and I'll cook you a hot dinner. But we won't stop serving the Lord."

The men vainly sought to resume their former ferocity, but the advantage had been taken away from them by the Christian charity of this courageous woman. The mob slowly disintegrated into confused units of twos and threes, which then departed, trying to cover their confusion with bluster. They did not carry out their threats: neither did they molest the worshippers again.[3]

Similar persecution was encountered by almost all of the young Pentecostal gatherings. W. C. Hoover met it in Chile. Newspaper reporters had begun to come to his services in search of sensational stories and Hoover found himself the center of some lurid publicity. One paper brought criminal action against him, accusing him of giving the people a "pernicious beverage to drink, called 'the Blood of the Lamb,' which produced a lethargy and the people fell on the floor."

Hoover quickly found himself in trouble with his superiors. His bishop tried to furlough him; Hoover refused to leave. In the end, Hoover was forced to withdraw from the Methodist Church and conduct his congregation as an independent.

The interesting thing is that persecution, far from destroying the Pentecostal movement, solidified small, uncertain groups and gave them a unity which otherwise they might never have achieved. The Camp Creek revival went on to become the Church of God, one of the largest Pentecostal denominations. The revival in Chile ultimately became the Methodist Pentecostal Church which today has a membership of over 600,000.

But in spite of its obvious futility, persecution of the Pentecostals continued. People seeking the reason for the unrelenting antagonism the Pentecostals inspired usually point to the "physical manifestations." Speaking in tongues, shouting, weeping, rolling on the floor, all seem to many to be a kind of emotionalism that is destructive of worship. But while these things might provoke distaste, they hardly account for the real anger the Pentecostals so often aroused. Dr. Van Dusen was probably closer to the heart of the matter when he asked the Anglican bishop where the Pentecostals' converts were coming from. Many came from the ranks of the heathen. But beyond a doubt many came straight from the pews of other churches.

Roman Catholics were especially hard hit. Dozens of Spanish-speaking Pentecostal congregations sprang up in New York. Among Catholics the rueful story went around that the Pentecostals had a new translation of the Bible. In the Catholic Bible Jesus' command to Peter was, "Feed my sheep!" But the Pentecostal version had it, "Steal my sheep!" And at sheep-stealing they had become masters.

Protestant churches were not exempt though. Government figures on the comparative growth of churches between 1926 and 1936 showed that during this period the traditional churches *lost* 2 million members: 8 per cent of their total. In the same period the Pentecostals showed:

> Pentecostal assemblies:  up 264.7%
> Assemblies of God:       up 208.7%
> Church of God:           up  92.8%

Where, people were suddenly asking, was all this burgeoning membership coming from—and could it have anything to do with the missing 2 million?

They asked themselves where their adherents were going, but not why they were going. What was it that the Pentecostals had to say that was so appealing? No one bothered to ask, and when the Pentecostals volunteered the information they did it in such a way as to antagonize. Pamphlet warfare broke out between the Pentecostals and any denomination deigning to answer back. Aggressive, evangelical, with a martyr's loyalty to his beliefs, the Pentecostal gained the reputation of tight narrowness: if you don't do it my way you're totally wrong. Most wrong of them all was the "liberal" who spent his time building beautiful churches and watering down the Gospel.

Rapidly the walls went up between the Pentecostals and the rest of Christendom. The traditional churches dismissed these tongues-speakers as devotees of a passing fad that would soon blow over. The Pentecostals dismissed the old-line churches as having lost touch with the dynamic power that was the Church's chief birthright.

Invisible to one another behind their walls, the two camps went their separate ways. There was no attempt by either to search out values in the other, no notion even that there were such values. For fifty years it was out of sight, out of mind. And then abruptly there was a change.

Chapter Six

# The Walls
# Come Tumbling Down

"How's the book going?" Tib asked. She was transferring dishes from the kitchen shelves into packing barrels that the moving company had provided.

"I don't know. . . ." I looked out the kitchen window at the bright June afternoon. "I'm sick of church squabbles. The last three books I got out of the library didn't tell me anything but how wrong everyone else is."

The fact was that now that the golfers were thick on the putting green which I watched from my attic window, the whole subject of religion and actual experience of God and mystic hospital visions seemed impossibly remote. I'd hoped, just for a moment a while back, that my explorations into the Pentecostal story might yield some personal answers too. Answers to the dryness in religious life that I felt and they apparently did not.

But it was becoming apparent that they had no answers, only fresh problems, and the book was becoming a chore rather than an adventure. The Pentecostals were only confused human beings, and I was another.

A Good Humor truck jangled up the street and as in a conjuring trick three faces appeared at the screen door.

"Can we—" Donn began.

"No," said Tib from deep inside a cupboard. "We're having ice cream for supper."

The faces disappeared.

We were moving so that everyone in the family could have a proper bedroom. Tib is a writer too, and together our offices took up the attic of the present small house. Downstairs were two bedrooms. Scott and Donn were in one, Elizabeth and the washing machine in the other, and Tib and I slept on a sofa-bed in the living room. Recently we'd found a larger house and moving day was two days off.

And I had to break the news that I'd just invited a key interview for the book up to dinner.

"Speaking of supper," I began—but Tib emerged from the cupboard still thinking about the research.

"I think I know what your trouble is," she said. "I think you've been spending too much time in the library and not enough time with people."

It was an opening made in heaven. "You're right!" I said heartily. "I agree completely. In fact, I've invited someone to spend the night."

The rattle of paper ceased abruptly. "You've what!"

"A preacher."

Tib's eyes traveled from the wood shavings on the kitchen floor to the boxes stacked in the living room.

"His name," I went on rapidly, "is David du Plessis. He's a South African. He's one of the most influential Pentecostals in the world today and he's only going to be in town overnight and. . . ."

Now she was eyeing me as though measuring me for a box of my own.

". . . and I've booked a room for him at the Kittle House."

I profited from her sigh of relief to add, "He knows we're

moving and he says he'd just as soon eat cold beans right out of a can."

"That's about what it will be," said Tib. But so skillfully had I conveyed my news that she gave me a smile of pure forgiveness as she said it.

From every side I'd heard the name David du Plessis. Apparently here was a man from as insular and defensive a background as anyone's who had suddenly, in mid-life, turned into an outgoing and communicative personality, who talked lovingly and not accusingly to people of other traditions. "There's a change taking place among Pentecostals," I was told. "If you want to know what it's all about, you really ought to meet David du Plessis." When I heard that he was going to be in New York I invited him out, moving week or no.

David du Plessis turned out to be the kind of person you called "David" right away. You could see the sparkle in his eyes even as he walked up the driveway. Within ten minutes after he entered our house, his suit coat was off and he was wrapping china.

"You've an expert helping you now," he said in the soft South African accent that sounds British to American ears. "My wife and I have moved so often that I pack dishes the way some men tie trout flies."

And that's the way we spent the rest of the afternoon, bending over packing barrels and talking. Tib was right: I hadn't been spending enough time with people. From David du Plessis I caught a glimpse of a Pentecostal world very different from the early days I had been reading about. The change had occurred in the space of a single lifetime, and David's own personal history was a case in point.

David du Plessis had had a role in the Pentecostal movement almost from its beginning. In 1908—just two years after Azusa Street—two Americans who had witnessed that revival arrived in Johannesburg, rented a long-abandoned Presbyterian church, and began to preach. Their message of the Baptism of the Holy Spirit with speaking in tongues was new in South Africa and from the beginning large crowds gathered to listen.

David's father was one of the people who dropped into the church out of curiosity. David was just nine years old at the time, but he can still remember the effect of that preaching on his father. "He acted like a man on fire," David recalls. "He wanted to leave his business right away and do something for the Lord." David's father was a carpenter by trade. Almost before the family knew it, they were out in the African bush, where his father built mission stations for Pentecostals who were carrying the message into the native territories.

David's family—and later David himself—came into the Pentecostal movement at a time when it was being severely ignored by the older churches. He grew up in an atmosphere charged with resentment and dislike. When, as a young adult, he decided to go into the Pentecostal ministry he knew who the enemies were: sin, the devil, and liberal churchmen.

David rose steadily in the Pentecostal movement. For twenty years after his ordination he stayed in Africa, preaching in a church of his own, working as editor for a Pentecostal newspaper, then acting as executive secretary of the Pentecostal Fellowships in South Africa. In time opportunities came for work in the international Pentecostal movement and he found himself in Geneva, Paris, London, Stockholm. By 1949 he was secretary-general of the World Conference of Pentecostal Fellowships. And in each job, he with the others contributed building blocks to the wall of misunderstanding separating the Pentecostals from the old-line churches.

Then David was in an automobile accident. The accident had a profound effect on him, on his ministry, and ultimately on the entire Pentecostal movement.

At the time of the accident, David was in the United States, making arrangements for the Second World Conference of Pentecostals which was to be held in Paris the summer of 1949. David, as executive secretary, had the responsibility for planning the conference from its broadest concept to its most minute detail.

"And I wasn't handling the job well," he recalls. "I was impatient when people's ideas differed from my own. I tended to see the issues in black and white, and to think of people as villains or heroes. I had come to my opinions the hard way—through experience—and refused even to listen to anyone whose experience pointed in a different direction. I was, in short, repeating on a small scale the same pattern that the whole Pentecostal movement was repeating on a large scale.

"Then, in one instant, all that was changed."

It was late at night and David was hurrying from one appointment to another in a hilly region of Tennessee. A friend, Paul Walker, had offered to drive him in the interest of time. The night was dark and rainy, clouds of fog hid the road. Conversation had almost ceased because of the late hour and the difficult driving. Suddenly Walker peered intently through the streaming windshield. David remembers him saying:

"There's supposed to be a white bridge . . ." but he never finished his sentence. Out of the fog suddenly loomed the hulk of a locomotive, stopped without lights directly across the highway.

Walker tried to brake his car, but the road was slick and the automobile skidded into the train.

Paul Walker was hurt only slightly. But David's head smashed through the windshield. He was jerked back through the glass, cutting himself both going and coming. His left leg was broken above the knee. His back was twisted, his shoulder cut.

Twelve hours later, David regained consciousness. His leg was in traction. His face—held together by thirty-seven stitches—was bandaged so tightly that he could not see. Yet something very strange was going on.

"When I came to," David remembers, "I felt as if I were waking from a good sleep. The doctor asked me:

" 'How are you, Preacher?'

" 'Just fine.' I told him.

"The doctor laughed, but I meant it."

After David had been in the hospital for a week other doctors came to ask questions. They were mystified. David didn't have a temperature. He ate normally. He slept normally without drugs. "You should be getting a reaction by now," one of the doctors said. "You should at least show a fever. You're an awfully sick man."

"Oh, but Doctor," David replied, "that's where you're wrong. I'm not sick. I'm only broken."

Although for different reasons, David was as puzzled about his condition as the doctors were. He began to wonder if there could be some hidden, God-given purpose behind the accident. The circumstances were peculiarly void of harm. Paul Walker had not been seriously hurt; the automobile had been adequately covered by insurance; even the hospital bills were settled by the railroad. And there was not the slightest pain.

"The only real effect of the accident," says David, "was to slow down my bullheaded, steamroller approach to the Paris conference. All of a sudden I had to let some of the arrangements out of my own hands. I had to ask for help both from other people and from God."

Over the next weeks, lying in his bed in the hospital, David wrote literally thousands of letters by dictating into a machine. Without deliberately trying, he noticed a subtle change in the tone of his letters, from one stoutly holding a position, to one that was "listening," as it were, for God's position, even when it meant listening to men who stood against him.

"The Conference that followed was a success, I suppose," says David. "But I do not think that was the main result of the accident. I found that I had gone through a tempering process. I was simply not the same man. I was now patient, kinder, softer spoken, whereas at the first World Conference I'd been hasty and loud and determined. The accident seemed to have moulded me to be the man God needed for a special situation."

David thought, at first, that the Conference itself was the special situation. And the Conference did indeed have a different spirit. But it was what happened afterwards that intrigued David. As the years passed he began to think more and more often about a group of people he had once summarily dismissed: those liberal churchmen who by his lights were taking the heart out of the Gospel. Why should they keep coming into his thoughts: surely God didn't intend him to become involved with the liberals. "Why, I'd never get past their secretaries," he argued. "I'd get nothing but cold shoulder, and I don't want to live on cold shoulder."

David has a habit of talking aloud this way when he prays. At its best he approaches a kind of dialogue with God, when guidance comes to him as a kind of interiorized voice. David has learned over the years to pay close attention to this voice. Now it came to him clearly, using the words of an old hymn. "Trust, and obey." Those seemed to be his orders.

The strange thing was that the trust seemed somehow concerned with those walls he and his fellow Pentecostals had built in an effort to defend the integrity of the Gospel. "Trust Me," God seemed to be saying. "Let the walls down. Hold out the hand of friendship to any who will take it." The impression was so clear that David could not ignore it. He would at least make the experiment. He would try going to the very headquarters of the most liberal, the most intellectual, the most ecumenically minded of modernists. To David this group was not hard to name: it would be the World Council of Churches.

"All right, Lord, if you say so," said David, picking up the telephone to call his travel agent for a ticket to New York. He was in Dallas, World Council headquarters were in New York. "I'll go to the World Council next Monday morning and just see what happens."

Immediately the inner voice spoke. "No, do not go on Monday. Ask for reservations on Thursday so that you can be in the offices of the World Council on Friday."

David thought a bit, then put down the phone. "Wait a minute now; here is something strange." He thought it over a little longer. "Why should I go there at the end of the week rather than Monday when everyone's fresh?"

"On Monday there will be nobody in the office."

David was still confused, but he went ahead and booked a flight for Thursday night. On Friday morning he walked into the offices of the Council in New York. He had made no appointments at all. He knew hardly any names of the men there. He did not know what he was supposed to say if he got to see them.

But in he went.

The young lady at the reception desk looked up. David explained who he was and then,

"Is—ah—Dr. Carpenter free?" he ventured, bringing up one of the few names he did know.

"No, I'm sorry, he isn't."

"Well, then," said David, "Dr. Barnes?"

"Sorry."

"Is there anyone at all in the office I could see?"

"No, sir, no one at all."

Well, there it was. It was the cold shoulder he'd expected all along. What wild notion had seized him, anyhow, to make him think it might be different? The word "Pentecostal" had always slammed doors in some circles, above all—

"They're all in conference just now," the receptionist continued. "But they should be through pretty soon, and then I imagine you can see whomever you'd like to." She glanced at the calendar on her desk and laughed. "This is the first day all week anyone's been here. I've been turning people away in droves. But they all came in for the meeting this morning, so you're in luck."

David sat down, feeling a little better about his guidance. He saw several people at the World Council that Friday, and they not only listened, they made notes as he talked, they picked up phones and read the notes to others, they paid attention.

It was the beginning. Ultimately, the tempering process of the accident propelled David through many strange new doors. He found himself being introduced to the very men he had spent a lifetime avoiding. One theologian would call another and introduce him. He was shunted from college to university to seminary.

"Which ones?" I asked.

"Well, let's see." He drew a well-worn appointment book from his pocket. "Here were a few dates last fall. October 27 I was at the Congregationalists' seminary in Myerstown, Pennsylvania. The next day, October 28, I was invited to speak at Yale University School of Divinity. And on October 30 and 31 I was with professors from Harvard, Yale, Union, Drew and Chicago at a special retreat in Greenwich, Connecticut. Then on November 2, I was at Princeton Theological. November 5 I went to Union Seminary in New York. . . ."

David put his datebook back in his pocket. "You know," he said, "something very peculiar was happening. I really *enjoyed* meeting these professors and scholars and churchmen. I, who haven't even finished the second year of college. I thought being around people like that would make me self-conscious: frightened lest I show my ignorance. But to my surprise I found myself relaxed and at ease. I never wrote out my lectures. I didn't even use notes. I simply made myself an instrument which the Spirit could use if He chose. And the interesting thing is that I was given powers of expression I do not normally possess."

At Seabury House, headquarters of the Episcopal church, David was asked the touchiest question of all—the one which in the past had led to more ill-will toward the Pentecostals than any other. He'd been talking to a group of clergymen for thirty minutes or so about the Pentecostal experience when one of the priests stood up suddenly and said with some asperity:

"Mr. du Plessis, are you telling us that you Pentecostals have the truth, and we other churches do not?"

David admits he prayed fast. "No," he said. "That is not what I mean." He cast about for a way to express the difference the Pentecostal feels exists between his church and others—a feeling so often misunderstood—and suddenly he found himself thinking about an appliance he and his wife had bought when they moved to their Dallas home.

"We both have the truth," he said. "You know, when my wife and I moved to America we bought a marvelous device called a deep freeze, and there we keep some rather fine Texas beef.

"Now my wife can take one of those steaks out and lay it, frozen solid, on the table. It's steak, all right, no question of that. You and I can sit around and analyze it: we can discuss its lineage, its age, what part of the steer it comes from. We can weigh it and list its nutritive values.

"But if my wife puts that steak on the fire, something different begins to happen. My little boy smells it from way out in the yard and comes shouting:

" 'Gee, Mom, that smells good! I want some!'

"Gentlemen," said David, "that is the difference between our ways of handling the same truth. You have yours on ice; we have ours on fire."

David was with us for twenty-four hours and left six months' worth of work behind him: I had filled page after page of a notebook with names and addresses of people not in the Pentecostal churches but in the denominations—Methodists, Baptists, Lutherans, Presbyterians—who had had the Baptism.

I could see that it was going to be a mammoth job contacting all these people. Just the mechanics of writing each one, for instance, took me three weeks. Then as replies began to come in there was the task of setting up interviews. Some I traveled to see, others had plans to be in New York themselves within the year. Some I interviewed over the telephone, some I got to know through correspondence. And with a few I experimented with a new technique: a conversation by tape recorder where I explained the nature of the book and asked questions on one side of a tape and they talked to me on the other.

Two of the people whom I got to know by telephone were Charles and Helen Maurice from Richmond, Virginia. As soon as he received my letter, Charles put in a long-distance call and, while I wondered guiltily what it was costing him, answered the entire list of questions I had asked in it. They were strangely reassuring people to know, perhaps because they were a suburban family with problems much like our own who happened, incidentally, to be very enthusiastic about the Baptism in the Holy Spirit.

"They have problems with their lawn," I told Tib.

Either Charles or his wife called frequently after that, with a fine disregard for end-of-the-month bills, just to inquire how the book was coming on, to offer me additional leads to tongues-speaking people whose names they thought I might not have.

Charles had a law office in Richmond, he told me, and was an Assistant District Attorney for the city. He and Helen were both so full of quiet good humor and the joy of living that I found myself wanting to meet them in person, and said so.

Charles thought for a moment. "Have you ever heard of

the Full Gospel Business Men's Fellowship International?"
he said.

"Say it again, slower."

"The F.G.B.M.F.I., for short. It's a group of business
and professional people from all denominations who've had or
are seeking the Baptism in the Holy Spirit and get together
several times a year to share experiences."

The F.G.B.M.F.I. was having its annual convention in
Atlantic City at the end of November, Charles said, and he
and Helen were going to be there. If Tib and I could come,
it would be a chance to meet one another.

"It's lively," he cautioned me. "But if you'll come with an
open mind, you'll never be the same."

"Sure," I said, little suspecting what I was agreeing to. "Put
us down and we'll see you there."

Thus casually the date was made. November 30, 1960.

The thing that made this research into tongues-speaking
among members of conventional churches difficult was the
element of secrecy which surrounded it. There were excep-
tions, like the Maurices, but for the most part, non-Pentecostal people who spoke in tongues guarded the fact like an
atomic formula. Typical of the replies to my letter in early
1960 was this one from a minister in a little town in the
Middle West:

I would be most happy to share with you any of my experiences
that would further the work of the Kingdom as the Holy Spirit
directs. At present however since there is only one other parsonage
family with whom I am in contact concerning the Holy Spirit
and His manifestations, I must request that my name not be used.

Again and again during the first few months of that year, I
would finish an interview with a Presbyterian, Baptist or
Methodist who had had the Baptism, only to have him say,
"Now you understand that this is all off the record."

Here and there, an article would appear on the subject, but never very personal, never naming names. The Episcopalian journal, *Living Church*, for example, ran an editorial which said, in part:

Speaking in tongues is no longer a phenomenon of some odd sect across the street. It is in our midst, and it is being practiced by clergy and laity who have stature and good reputation in the Church. Its widespread introduction would jar against our esthetic sense and some of our most strongly entrenched preconceptions. But we know that we are members of a Church which definitely needs jarring—if God had chosen this time to dynamite what Bishop Sterling of Montana has called "Episcopalian respectabilianism" we know of no more terrifyingly effective explosive.[1]

And then the explosive went off. An event occurred which suddenly thrust tongues into the headlines, and ripped the curtain of secrecy away. It happened in a large Episcopal church in Van Nuys, California.

Father Dennis Bennett was a successful man. Born in London, educated at the University of Chicago and Chicago Theological Seminary, Father Bennett took over struggling St. Mark's Episcopal Church in Van Nuys in 1953. Under his leadership the church grew steadily until it had a membership of 2600 and a staff of four clergymen.

But there was something missing, Father Bennett felt, in his own personal religious life. When he was eleven years old he had had a conversion experience which had left him with a memory of warmth and love he had rarely been able to approach again.

Then, one day in the summer of 1959, Father Bennett received a call from a fellow priest, Frank Maguire, of Monterey Park, California. Father Maguire had become quite puzzled by events which were taking place in his church: two of his parishioners—recently dropped from the church's lists as inactive—had reappeared on the scene and were showing remarkable signs of an extremely vigorous faith.

Father Maguire was impressed. Nevertheless, he felt vaguely uneasy about certain phrases which kept coming into their conversation such as "Baptism in the Holy Spirit," and "speaking in tongues."

"I think these people have some kind of extra dividend which they are overemphasizing," Frank Maguire told Dennis Bennett. "But I'd like you to come visit them with me, and help me evaluate what's going on." Thus began a three-month-long investigation of the experience by the two priests. By mid-November, 1959, both men were being drawn toward the experience themselves.

"There's only one thing," said Father Bennett. "I'd like the Baptism without the tongues."

"Sorry, Father," he was told. "But the tongues come with the package. This is how it happened to us, and we don't know of any other way."

Dennis Bennett was prayed for and received the Baptism on November 14, and Frank Maguire on November 17.

As people in Bennett's church asked him about a change they noticed in him, he told them what had happened. Over a period of months some seventy members of his parish asked for and received the Baptism. They were key people in the church: the junior warden, the president of the women's guild, the curate. And those who had been so baptized were enthusiastic about the experience.

Others, however, felt differently. Of the four priests in the parish, two had now received the Baptism and two had not. The two who had not were deeply opposed to the idea and soon had a following of others who felt the same. A serious rift was being created in the church, and Father Bennett saw that something would have to be done. On April 3, 1960, Father Bennett preached a sermon on his experience. So that there would be no part of the church "out of the know," he told the whole story, including the fact that he had spoken in a language which he could not understand. This was **too** much for many. One of the associate priests in the middle of the service took off his vestments and announced that under the circumstances he had no choice but to resign. After the service the church treasurer suggested to Father Bennett that it might be more appropriate for him to resign. He did.

Newspapers carried the story the next day. The wire services picked it up. Overnight the story swept the country: speaking in tongues had appeared in a decent, ordinary church and had caused strife, division and dissention. *Time* carried the story. So did *Newsweek*.

My first reaction was that this confirmed, in 1960, what the history of the Pentecostals had already made me suspect. Tongues made people fight. Bishop Francis Eric Bloy of Los Angeles issued a pastoral letter banning the use of tongues under church auspices. Father Bennett was shunted off to Seattle where he was put in charge of a tiny mission church. It looked to me like a pretty clear effort to get a trouble-maker out of the way. I wrote Father Bennett at his new address, told him about the book I was writing, and asked for his version of what had happened at Van Nuys.

Back came a reply, written without the aid of a secretary. "Please excuse typing errors," he began, "I am doing this myself, and I am a very poor and erratic typist!" I scanned the letter quickly, expecting to find in it the clue to the personality that had caused strife, division and dissention in Van Nuys. I found none. Father Bennett made only passing reference to Van Nuys: his whole attention was on the job to be done in Seattle.

The response of the Episcopal Church in this area to my witness re the Holy Spirit and Tongues has been tremendous, and I have been kept busy night and day. Not less thrilling has been the coming back to life of the little St. Luke's Church which I took over last July. Fifty now have the Baptism in the Holy Spirit in this little Mission. Some fourteen Priests of this Diocese have now received the Gift of Tongues. So Praise the Lord!

Nowhere—not once—in the long correspondence that developed between me and Father Bennett did he complain about any ill-treatment he had received, nor lash out at people who disagreed with him. Much later I met him in New York, and found the same true of him in person. He was quiet and composed in spite of an aura about him of immense energy, a man so filled with the significance of today that he had no time to rehash the events of yesterday. In his only reference to past events, he said once:

"I have, of course, tried to figure out just why we at Van Nuys were singled out for all this sensational publicity when hundreds of other churches across the country are having the Baptism appear in their midst with no trouble at all.

"The only conclusion I have reached is that God wanted people to speak up about their experience with the Holy Spirit. We'd all been pretty quiet before Van Nuys. Now, I think, people are going to begin to share their stories."

It was true. Suddenly I could scarcely keep up with the flood of mail from people who wanted to tell me their experiences and sign their names to them. They wrote from everywhere. The entire ministerial staff of a sedate Presbyterian church in suburban New Jersey received the Baptism. Eighty-five per cent of the membership of a Baptist church in the same state received the Baptism. In Wheaton, Illinois, members of Trinity Episcopal Church received the Baptism.

Students at Princeton, Yale, Harvard, U.C.L.A., Stanford, Wheaton, began to hold prayer meetings where the Baptism was sought, and received. At Yale, for example, twenty men including a faculty member, five deacons of the University Chapel, a Phi Beta Kappa, and Summa Cum Laude graduate student received the Baptism and began to practice Spirit-filled prayer.

My research had indicated that in the early days the Pentecostal movement tended to draw most heavily on semi-educated or unskilled people. Now, just glancing over a part of my correspondence file I noted this interesting breakdown of occupations:

| | | |
|---|---|---|
| mathematician | F.B.I. agent | attorney |
| psychiatrist | registered nurse | porter |
| doctor | automobile agency | State Department |
| police captain | owner | official |
| dentist | psychologist | oil magnate |
| real estate agent | Hollywood | Jewish rabbi |
| housewife | photographer | restauranteur |
| minister | actor | surveyor |
| dairyman | airplane | biologist |
| tool and dye | manufacturer's | professor |
| manufacturer | wife | headmaster |
| salesman | I.C.B.M. engineer | |

More and more church leaders were coming out with statements on the Pentecostal movement within their own denominations:

■*The Rev. Samuel M. Shoemaker:* "Whatever the old-new phenomenon of 'speaking in tongues' means, it is amazing that it should break out, not only in Pentecostal groups, but among Episcopalians, Lutherans, and Presbyterians. I have not had this experience myself. I have seen people who have, and it has blessed them and given them power they did not have before. I do not profess to understand this phenomenon. But I am fairly sure it indicates the Holy Spirit's presence in a life, as smoke from a chimney indicates a fire below. I do know it means God is trying to get through into the Church, staid and stuffy and self-centered as it often is, with a kind of power that will make it radiant and exciting and self-giving. We should seek to understand and be reverent toward this phenomenon, rather than to ignore or scorn it." [2]

■*Dr. James I. McCord*, president of Princeton Theological Seminary: "Ours must become the Age of the Spirit, of God active in the world, shaking and shattering all our forms and structures, and bringing forth responses consonant with the Gospel and the world's need." [3]

■*Harvard's Dr. Ernest Wright:* ". . . the consummation of the Kingdom of God is to be marked by a great revival of the charismatic happenings. Both leaders and people will then be Spirit-filled and Spirit-empowered on a scale hitherto unknown." [4]

■*Billy Graham:* "In the main denominations we have looked a bit askance at our brethren from the Pentecostal churches because of their emphasis on the doctrine of the Holy Spirit, but I believe the time has come to give the Holy Spirit His rightful place in our churches. We need to learn once again what it means to be Baptized with the Holy Spirit." [5]

Overseas, the Church of England was taking notice too:

■*Bishop Lesslie Newbigin* in his book, *The Household of God*, listed three principal streams of life within the Christian Church. The first is Catholic. The second is Protestant. And the third is Pentecostal.

■*Dr. Philip Edgcumbe Hughes*, editor of the Anglican theological quarterly *The Churchman*, visited California where he had heard that Episcopalians were speaking in tongues. Before leaving England, he had attributed this to "a flirtation under the hot California sun with the extravagances of Pentecostalism." But he came away with the opposite opinion. "The breath of the living God," he wrote, "is stirring among the dry bones of the major, respectable, old-established denominations and particularly in the Episcopalian Church." [6]

With the election of Pope John to the papacy, a new emphasis on Pentecost began to be evident within the Roman Catholic Church. Pope John constantly referred to the Vatican Council as a New Pentecost. And by the term he meant a Pentecost with the same charismatic manifestations of the Spirit long displayed in the Pentecostal churches, including speaking in tongues. The *Catholic Messenger*, discussing news coming out of the Council, defined this word "charism" that was popping up with such increased frequency in Catholic circles:

So it looks like we'll have to add charism to our vocabulary, because the news out of Rome right now is that it's one of the biggest stories of the Council.

Charism comes from a Greek word [the article went on], meaning literally a gift of love. As used by theologians, it describes a special talent freely bestowed by the Holy Spirit on an individual for the benefit of others rather than for his personal benefit. . . . In this vein, Cardinal Suenens of Belgium told his fellow Fathers that we must today recognize the existence of charisms for a balanced view of the Church, seeing them not as accidental additions, but as part of its nature.[7]

Father Daniel J. O'Hanlon, professor of theology at Alma College, Los Gatos, California, wrote an article for *America*, the national Catholic weekly, in which he said:

Few Catholics regard Pentecostals with more than amusement, if they take notice of their existence at all. Even most Protestants keep their distance from these unconventional Christians and find it difficult to say anything good about them. Nevertheless, the rapid growth of the Pentecostal movement all over the world and the extraordinary appeal it has for the kind of people to whom our Lord especially addressed himself, the poor and dispossessed, should warn us to put aside our squeamish bourgeois prejudices and take a long, hard look at it.

How are Catholics to get this look? Father O'Hanlon makes a suggestion unusual in his church.

The best, if not the only, way of getting to know what the Pentecostals are like is to visit their services, even though for most Catholics this means crossing over to visit a strange new world. Those who do come to know them at first hand will find much to admire and possibly even a few things to imitate.[8]

The reports on my desk pile up.

News comes that an Episcopal bishop, the Rt. Rev. Chandler W. Sterling, has received the Baptism. Students at Oregon State University are holding Spirit-filled prayer meetings. So are members of Holy Innocents' Parish, Corte Madera, California. Ivan S. Gamble, the pastor of the First Presbyterian Church of Prince Rupert, B.C., Canada, tells his congregation that he has received the Holy Spirit, and that his life has been transformed. David du Plessis accepts an invitation to preach from the pulpit of the Episcopal Cathedral in Detroit.

Dr. John Peters, Methodist minister and president of World Neighbors, receives the Baptism when a Baptist minister prays for him. Every Saturday a Spirit-filled prayer group meets in a room at the Benjamin Franklin Hotel in Philadelphia. The Pentecostal experience comes to Zion Lutheran Church, Glendive, Montana, and to Trinity Lutheran Church, San Pedro, California. The editor of the American Baptist Convention publication, *Frontier*, is filled with the Spirit. The *Lutheran Standard*, and the *Christian Advocate*, official publications of the Lutheran and Methodist churches, cover the news of the Pentecostal movement within their denominations; in tone the articles are cautious, but not hostile. The experience comes to the Casa Linda Methodist Church in the big town of Dallas, Texas, and to the Episcopal Church of the Advent in little Alice, Texas. It comes to Presbyterians of coal-region towns, like Alpine, Tennessee. And of the inner-city, like the Hillside Presbyterian Church of Jamaica, Long Island, New York.

On and on. The tide swells. After some sixty-five years, the Pentecostal revolution is at the gates.

# Chapter Seven

# A Visit from Lydia

But if we were living in the middle of a revolution, it was hard to find the way in which it touched our daily lives. Our new lawn was all hills; I went to the end-of-season sales and priced power mowers. Tib got out the kids' winter clothes and went through the annual trauma of discovering that nothing fitted.

A letter came in the mail from the Full Gospel Business Men's Fellowship International. Reservations for two had been made in our name for the convention two months away: would we please send in our check. Charles Maurice had not forgotten. His enthusiasm over the long distance line in the spring had made the convention sound interesting; but now the whole thing looked deadly dull, and I was sorry we'd gotten involved. I put the letter in my "To Do" folder, along with an ad for a reduced-rate subscription to a magazine I wasn't much interested in. Both were suggestions I might follow up on. Some day.

I was taking the train into town almost daily now. I'd decided to get some tape recordings of people speaking in tongues, with the idea of playing them back for some language experts and seeing what they made of it all. Our home in Chappaqua was too far to ask people to come to, and so I was holding the recording sessions at *Guideposts'* office in New York City.

The *Guideposts* staff had gotten quite accustomed to the energetic Pentecostal personalities coming in to talk on the tape machine. The first time the receptionist was greeted with a resounding, "Good morning, sister! Is Brother Sherrill in?" her answer had a chilly edge to it. But before long she was "brother"-ing and "sister"-ing with the best of them, and actually looking forward to these little explosions in the routine office day.

For the actual recording I would take my visitor into a private office where the machine was set up, and shut the door. If I hoped by this to insulate the rest of the office from distracting sounds, it was a wasted gesture. Pentecostals are notably unself-conscious about tongues. The volume of sound would swell, strange syllables and rhythms would pour from the little room where my guest and I sat, and from the hush in the outer office I could tell that all activity had ceased and every ear was tuned to the closed door.

Tongues became a favorite topic of conversation at coffee breaks, replacing even the World Series in liveliness. The reactions of the various typists and editors seemed to range from amusement to hilarity. My birthday rolled around and beside the traditional cake with which the office honors such occasions, I found a small package. Inside was a miniature Greek vase with a long inscription in Greek characters running around the rim.

"It's Greek to us, John," read the note tied to the neck, "but keep recording. Happy Birthday."

The ribbing was always in fun. But I thought it expressed, too, the serious doubts which many at the office were feeling about this phenomenon, and which I certainly shared. Dina Donohue, our departments editor, summed it up for us all one rainy noon when we'd had sandwiches sent in from the delicatessen. As we sat around the table in the outer office, Dina announced,

"I can speak in tongues too. Listen."

And off she went: strange grunts and clicks and nonsense syllables, delivered with much expression and all remarkably language-like. There was a round of applause for Dina's fluency, but in the silence which followed my secretary said,

"Do you really mean to say you can tell a difference between what Dina just did and these 'tongues' these people claim to be speaking?"

And I had to admit that I personally could not.

Wasn't that the whole problem in a nutshell? Not that tongues-speakers were trying to deceive anybody, but that they had utterly deceived themselves. Under the stress of religious emotion and with a strong tradition leading them to expect certain happenings, weren't they mistaking for the workings of God Himself, a simple gibberish such as anyone could manufacture?

It was while these thoughts were strongest in my mind that I had a visit from Lydia.

I'd heard of Lydia Maxam from several different people. Aristocratic was the word most frequently used to describe her. She was a Philadelphia Main Liner, an Episcopalian, and one of the few non-Pentecostals who had agreed to talk in tongues into my tape recorder.

I liked Lydia the minute she walked into the office: tall, dignified, smiling. "There's a condition on my agreeing to talk into that apparatus," she said when we were alone in the little room and I had explained the workings of the recorder. "To me, tongues are always prayer. A special kind of prayer, too. I use them when I'm praying about a problem to which my own mind has no solution—usually a prayer for somebody else when I can't possibly know all the factors and complications.

"So if you want me to speak in tongues, you'll have to let me pray about some real problem—preferably one that concerns you, or someone close to you."

I thought for a moment. There was nothing really pressing— and then I remembered Tib's manuscript. This was a magazine story on which she'd been working for weeks. Version after version had ended up in the wastepaper basket, and that morning she'd told me, as near to tears as I'd ever seen her over her work, that the deadline was tomorrow and she felt no closer to a solution than the day she'd accepted the assignment.

I described the situation to Lydia. "Is that the kind of thing you mean?"

"Exactly," she said. "If your wife were here, I'd ask her to sit there in that chair. Then I'd simply place my hands on her head, and ask the Holy Spirit to use me as a channel through which to enter this situation. I'd ask Him to remove whatever distractions or personal problems were blocking the perfect understanding which is one of His gifts. I'd ask Him to take over this story to His own glory. Tongues would simply be a token of yielding my will and understanding to His."

In the absence of the person for whom the prayer was offered, Lydia said, someone else could sit in for her. Would I sit in the chair in Tib's stead and receive the prayer on her behalf? I agreed, and right away was sorry. Wouldn't I be terribly conscious of all those listening ears outside the door? How could I go along personally with something about which I had such mixed feelings?

But it was too late to back out. I turned on the recorder, placed the chair at the window, as far from the door as it would go, and sat down. And immediately was faced with something worse than listeners. Looking right into my window was a dress manufacturer's loft where about fifteen girls sat at sewing machines and seemed, it suddenly occurred to

me, singularly disinterested in their work. Our two windows
had stared at each other for many years; this was the first time
the fact had ever bothered me.

Lydia, however, seemed oblivious to our surroundings. She
stepped behind my chair, laid both hands lightly on my head,
and began to pray, in English, for the healing of whatever was
blocking Tib's creativity. One of the girls in the loft glanced
our way. She said something to the girl at the next machine
and now they were both looking at us. I closed my eyes to
shut out distracting influences but this made it worse, for now
in my mind's eye the entire factory staff was gathered at the
window staring at the elegant lady praying over the guy with
the balding top.

The humor in the situation was too much for me. I started
to laugh, but swallowed it because Lydia was praying with
such obvious sincerity. And it was at this moment, while I was
still struggling with laughter, that an extraordinary thing happened.

With no change in the tone of her voice, Lydia began to
pray in tongues. And at that instant I *felt*—actually felt—a
wave of warmth pass from her hands into my head and then
swiftly down through my chest and arms. The sensation was
of heat, but without the effect of heat: I didn't feel flushed or
hot. It was like coming close to some immense source of heat,
a blast furnace or a sun, which had no burning quality whatever.

This lasted all the while Lydia's prayer in tongues continued, though the sensation was not so intense after the first
moment. And suddenly I discovered that I was crying. Huge
tears were rolling down my face and plopping onto my neck-
tie. The tears were no more related to my emotions than the
heat I had been feeling was related to the radiator in the wall.
I was acutely conscious of the girls in the next building: I
didn't dare open my eyes for fear of meeting theirs. As Lydia

continued to pray I grew more and more self-conscious. When at last she finished and lifted her hands from my head, I swung the swivel chair sharply away from the window and busied myself for a long time with the tape machine. In the outer office typewriters abruptly started clacking .

Lydia left a short time afterward, as cool and poised as though we'd been discussing the opening of the ballet season, but I stayed alone in my small office most of the day. I had a lot to ponder, a lot to sort out in my thoughts. I felt like a man who had stooped to pet a kitten and finds his hand on a tiger. What was the palpable power that had invaded this room with Lydia's prayer in tongues? Was it possible that I'd been wrongly looking at this phenomenon as a mere incidental to something else? Did it have, in and of itself, some mysterious power?

Tib met me at the train station that evening, a cat-that-ate-the-canary look on her face.

"How's the manuscript?" I said, as I slid behind the wheel.

"Mailed!" she said, moving over for me. "I dropped it in the box coming down. I don't know why on earth I had such trouble with that story. It was so simple, when I finally did it! I'd been trying to make it so complicated. I sat down to it this noon and there it was, right before my nose. It almost wrote itself."

I didn't tell her about Lydia's prayer. I didn't know how to go about telling her. Before I did any more talking it was obvious I was going to have to do a lot more thinking, a lot more digging, a lot more investigating.

After dinner that night I wrote down three questions to which I wanted answers:

Does the Bible say anything about tongues having strange powers?

If they do have power, why did they fall out of use for so many centuries?

Do people who use tongues today report this power?

I started with the Bible. I got out my concordance the next morning and discovered that the New Testament contains some thirty references to tongues. But even the most cursory listing of them showed me that the Bible was talking about two very distinct *uses* of this phenomenon.

The first use was the one with which I was already familiar: where tongues are considered a *sign* that the Holy Spirit has entered a certain believer. The tongue seems to have little importance in itself; it is valued only as evidence of something else.

This use of tongues is first spoken of—at least in order of appearance in the Bible—in the Gospel of Mark. Jesus has been crucified, has risen from the dead, and now appears to His disciples with instructions to preach the gospel all over the world. "And these signs shall accompany them that believe," He tells them, ". . . they shall speak with new tongues. . . ." [1]

As the words of Christ Himself, this passage of course has great authority and Pentecostals set much store by it. I soon discovered, however, that not everybody accepted it as equally authentic. The King James translation of the Bible was made from a manuscript called the Codex Alexandrinus which dated from the fifth century and contained this verse. Earlier manuscripts, dating from the fourth century, however, do not contain the verse. Of course in the fourth Christ's words may have been part of an oral tradition, not yet set down in writing. Perhaps the consistent experience of a large group of Christians convinced them that this tradition belonged as part of the written heritage of the Church.

The book of Acts, written toward the end of the first century, and which no one has suspected of later additions, refers several times to tongues as a sign of the Holy Spirit's presence. Three things, I thought, were worth noting about these references.

1 Tongues were accepted as incontestable proof that the Holy Spirit had come upon a given person or group of people. "The believers who had come with Peter, men of Jewish birth, were astonished that the gift of the Holy Spirit should be poured even on Gentiles. *For they could hear them speaking in tongues. . . .*" [2]

2 It was equally uncontested that tongues were the result of the Spirit Himself speaking through men. "And they were all filled with the Holy Spirit and began to talk in other tongues, *as the Spirit gave them power of utterance.*" [3]

3 The tongues themselves excited very little notice. When Peter was summing up his experience in Caesarea for the church in Jerusalem he didn't bother to mention tongues at all, although they had been a salient part of the happenings there. [4]

So far, tongues have been treated as a sign of the Holy Spirit's coming. But when I turned to Paul's letters it was obvious that he was looking at them very differently. Paul was discussing tongues not as a one-time outpouring, but as a continuing experience. They were important not only as proof of God's presence, but because their use conferred certain benefits on the Church. They were a gift of the Spirit for the advantage of believers, to be used, along with the eight other gifts, for the upbuilding of God's people. In Paul's view, there seemed to be three principal ways in which tongues were of value:

1 In private prayer, tongues aided the speaker to praise God.
2 They let him pray even at those times when he was not sure what to ask for.
3 And in public worship, when accompanied by another of the nine Gifts, "interpretation," tongues provided a vehicle of direct communication between God and man.

This first letter to the Corinthians was written around 54 A.D. Paul was living in Ephesus when word came to him that the church in Corinth was in trouble. Among the irregularities and abuses that had crept into Christian practice was a kind of confused disorder at public worship, the result of misusing some of the Gifts of the Spirit, especially tongues. The twelfth, thirteenth and fourteenth chapters of his letter are devoted to a discussion of these gifts with considerable emphasis given to tongues. But in the process of cautioning Christians not to misuse their spiritual gifts, Paul left us with quite a clear picture of how they should be used. I went through the three chapters and made notes:

■I noticed first of all Paul's attitude toward the happenings in Corinth. There was no suggestion of surprise, no overtone of What's-going-on-over-there! He was obviously quite familiar with the various phenomena being reported. He accepts them without discussion as a genuine part of the Christian experience, and is concerned only that they be put into proper perspective.

■Paul considers the Holy Spirit to be the source of tongues. "To each is given the manifestation of the Spirit for the common good. To one is given through the Spirit the utterance of wisdom ... to another various kinds of tongues, to another the interpretation of tongues." [5]

■He believes their use is appointed by God. "And God has appointed in the church ... speakers in various kinds of tongues." [6]

■But he sees tongues as only one of many gifts which the Spirit manifests. He lists nine of these:
    –the word of wisdom
    –the word of knowledge
    –faith
    –gifts of healing
    –workings of miracles
    –prophecy
    –discerning of spirits
    –divers kinds of tongues
    –interpretation of tongues [7]

■Paul considers that all the gifts, including tongues, are given for a reason. "In each of us the Spirit is manifested ... for some useful purpose." [8]

▪In the case of tongues, the purpose is the strengthening of the one who uses them. "He that speaketh in a tongue edifieth himself. . . ." [9]

▪And, when accompanied by interpretation, they are also effective in building up the Church as a whole. "When you come together, each one has . . . a tongue, or an interpretation. Let all things be done for edification." [10]

▪But tongues are not among the highest and most important gifts. Paul places them at the bottom of the list: ". . . God has appointed in the church first apostles, second prophets, third teachers, then workers of miracles, then . . . speakers in various kinds of tongues." [11]

▪Paul regards tongues as a form of prayer. "For if I pray in a tongue. . . ." [12]

▪He associates this form of prayer chiefly with praise and thanksgiving. "Suppose you are praising God in the language of ecstacy. . . ." [13]

▪He also sees tongues (letter to the Romans) as a way to pray when the mind is perplexed. "In the same way the Spirit comes to the aid of our weakness. W do not even know how we want to pray, but through our inarticulate groans the Spirit himself is pleading for us, and God who searches our inmost being knows what the Spirit means, because he pleads for God's own people in God's own way. . . ." [14]

▪He is not talking theoretically, but from personal experience. He himself uses tongues extensively. "I thank God, I speak with tongues more than you all." [15]

▪He not only prays in tongues, but sings in tongues too. "I will sing with the Spirit, and I will sing with the understanding also." [16]

▪He does not expect that the language spoken will be recognized by the listeners. (Unlike Pentecost when each hearer recognized his own native dialect.) "For one who speaks in a tongue speaks not to men but to God; for no one understands him. . . ." [17]

▪He does not believe that the ministry of tongues is given to everyone. "Do all speak in tongues?" [18] The context here requires a negative answer. No, all do not speak in tongues. Pentecostals point out that in these three chapters Paul is discussing tongues as a gift only, not tongues as the initial *sign* of the Baptism in the Holy Spirit. They believe that everyone does speak in tongues, however briefly, at the moment of his Baptism, whether or not he is subsequently given the gift of tongues for use in his daily Christian living.

■Although sounding warnings as to their abuse, Paul does enjoin the Corinthians to speak in tongues. "Now I would have you all speak with tongues. . . ." [19] And ". . . forbid not to speak with tongues." [20]

If then two manifestations of tongues, both the sign and the gift, were known to the authors of the New Testament, and if along with them went such obvious advantages, why did tongues ever disappear from the Church?

To this second of my questions I found an immediate answer: They didn't.

Tongues continued to play a part in Christian experience down through the centuries. They were de-emphasized— probably as a result of such warnings as Paul sounded. People who experienced them kept so quiet about them that it is easy to miss the references to them altogether. But the minute I looked for them, there they were.

Way back in the second half of the second century, some Christians were complaining that the Church had lost its contagious fire. A revival led by Montanus urged Christians to look for a new Pentecost and to expect the same manifestations that had accompanied the first.

At first Montanism was well received. Two of the most respected and influential of the early Church Fathers, Tertullian and Irenaeus, found in the movement much that needed saying and gave it their support. But as tongues and other charismatic phenomena increased, Rome feared excess. Montanism was branded heretical and even the influence of Tertullian and Irenaeus could not soften the charge.

There were, however, other instances of charisma which were not so branded.

In the fourth century, St. Pachomius, who founded the first Christian monastery, was reported able to speak in both Greek and Latin, neither of which had he learned.

This mysterious ability to speak in an unlearned language crops up again in the fourteenth century in the experience of St. Vincent Ferrer.

And in the sixteenth century, St. Francis Xavier received the gift. St. Francis was one of the first Jesuit missionaries, preaching among the Indians and among the Japanese. He was reported able to preach in languages he had never learned.

Tongues appear at the beginning of many of the great revivals. The early Waldensians spoke in unknown languages. So did the Jansenists, and the Quakers and the Shakers and the Methodists. "While waiting upon the Lord," wrote W. C. Braithwaite in an account of early Quaker meetings, "we received often the pouring down of the Spirit upon us and ... we spoke with new tongues."

Beginning with the nineteenth century, I found both more original source materials in the library and more references to tongues.

■*Scotland, 1830*: Mary Campbell, a young girl from Fernicarry, is planning to become a missionary. One night, while praying with a group of friends, Miss Campbell begins to speak in a language unknown to her. She assumes, at first, that it is a language which will help her in her missionary work, but she is never able to identify it.

■*England, 1834*: A young and fashionable London minister of the Presbyterian church, Edward Irving, finds and encourages glossolalia in his church.

■*United States, 1854*: A certain V. P. Simmons reports glossolalia in New England. "In A.D. 1854 Elder F. G. Mathewson spoke in tongues and Elder Edward Burnham interpreted the same."

■*United States, c. 1855:* The Mormons speak in tongues at their colony in Nauvoo, Illinois. The seventh Article of Faith of the Latter-Day Saints states that they "believe in the gift of tongues, prophecy, revelation, visions, healing, interpretation of tongues."

■*Russia, c. 1855:* Deep in Czarist Russia, Pentecostal manifestations are reported in the Greek Orthodox Church.

■*England, 1873:* Tongues appear in the wake of the preaching campaigns of Dwight L. Moody. "When I got to the rooms of the YMCA," writes Robert Boyd after Moody had visited Sunderland, England, "I found the meeting on fire. The young men were speaking in tongues and prophesying. What on earth did it mean? Only that Moody had been addressing them that afternoon."

■*United States, 1875:* R. B. Swan, a pastor in Providence, R.I., writes, "In the year 1875 our Lord began to pour out upon us His Spirit: my wife and I with a few others began to utter a few words in the 'unknown tongue.'"

■*United States, 1879:* In Arkansas, W. Jethro Walthall speaks in tongues. "I knew nothing of the Biblical teaching about the Baptism or speaking in tongues," he writes.

■*Armenia, 1880:* Among Armenian Presbyterians in Kara Kala there is a strong Pentecostal movement, with speaking in tongues.

■*Switzerland, 1880:* Maria Gerber reports that in moments of special joy, which she describes as, "yielding my unruly heart to the Spirit," she sang spiritual songs in a language which she never learned. Later, Maria came to America, unable to speak English. One day while praying for a sick friend, her words, to the astonishment of them both, emerged as flawless English.

The difference between these random occurrences of tongues and the Pentecostal movement which began with the twentieth century, seemed to be that before Charles Parham and his Bible school at Stone's Folly, no one attached any significance to tongues. There was no attempt to persuade others to do likewise, no evangelistic fervor in the wake of the experience. Tongues remain isolated, haphazard, unremarked. But remain they do.

Chapter Eight

# Why Should Anyone Want
# to Speak in Tongues?

The third thing I had set myself to do after Lydia's visit was to talk to every tongues-speaker I knew and find out whether he believed that the practice somehow added a dimension to his life that ordinary English prayer did not. I still remembered that mysterious flow of heat from Lydia's hands—and the fact that when I got home the prayer she had said for Tib had been answered. Were these things just coincidence, and maybe a little imagination on my part, or did other people have similar experiences?

Of course when I asked Pentecostals what tongues did for them, the first answer was always, "Assure me that I have been baptized in the Holy Ghost." It was this assurance that Parham and his students were seeking when they began their long Bible study, and of course it would be a priceless asset in a believer's life: to know without question that God's own Spirit was manifested from within one. Pentecostals believe that tongues do provide this assurance; indeed it is a matter of dogma with them that the Baptism in the Holy Spirit is always accompanied with tongues.

"The Baptism of believers in the Holy Ghost," says the constitution of the Assemblies of God, "is witnessed by the initial physical sign of speaking with other tongues as the Spirit of God gives them utterance." The Declaration of Faith of the Church of God says essentially the same thing: "We believe in speaking with other tongues as the Spirit gives utterance, and that it is the initial evidence of the Baptism in the Holy Ghost."

Outside of the Pentecostal denominations, however, I found that people were not so sure—even those who had spoken in tongues at the moment of Baptism themselves.

A Lutheran minister, Larry Christenson, pastor of Trinity Church, San Pedro, California expresses what is probably the view of most non-Pentecostal tongues-speakers. Reviewing the accounts of the Baptism in the book of Acts, he asked,

Does this mean that everyone who receives the Holy Spirit will speak in tongues—and that if you have not spoken in tongues you have not really received the Holy Spirit? I do not believe that you can make such a case from Scripture. However, I do believe that the book of Acts suggests to us a helpful *pattern*: 1) Receiving the Holy Spirit is a definite, clear-cut, instantaneous experience. . . . 2) A simple and God-appointed way for you objectively to manifest the gift of the Holy Spirit is to lift up your voice in faith, and speak out in a new tongue at the prompting of the Holy Spirit.[1]

And at the opposite extreme from the Pentecostals are people who are convinced they have had the Baptism in the Holy Spirit but deny that tongues are a normal part of the experience at all. One of these is Dr. E. Stanley Jones. Tib and I talked to this veteran missionary to India about his feelings on the subject and later received a letter from him in which he told us about an experience he'd had while attending Asbury College in Wilmore, Kentucky.

"I was in a prayer meeting in the room of one of my fellow students," Dr. Jones wrote, "with three or four others with no special emotion or expectancy when suddenly and sovereignly we were all filled with the Holy Spirit—literally swept off our feet. I did not sleep the rest of the night, I could only walk the floor and praise Him. For three days no classes were held, all were turned into prayer meetings. People coming from the countryside were converted before they would get into the auditorium. They would drop on their knees on the campus and be converted. There was no preaching, only praying and testifying to release and victory. Every student on the campus was converted.

"I wondered what it meant. Then I soon found out. I was prepared by this visitation for my life's work. I found myself saying 'Yes' to my call as a missionary.

"The evidences of the Holy Spirit? The Holy Spirit Himself was the evidence. No other evidence was needed or wanted. To ask for evidence would be like asking for the evidence of the sun at midday. No one spoke in tongues, for it was not taught."

So here was the gamut of opinion on the importance of tongues in determining the Spirit's presence: from "essential" to "helpful" to "unnecessary."

But tongues were reputed to have other uses than simply to serve as a sign of the Baptism. When St. Paul was talking about tongues as a gift, he related them to the ability to praise God.

We had an interesting opportunity to compare this function of tongues in contemporary experience when we talked with a young Yale graduate. Robert V. Morris had been a member of the Yale Christian Fellowship, and had found his religious life fairly complete with the exception of this area of praise. He remembers interrupting himself one evening at a meeting of the YCF when it was his turn to lead the prayers. He was using a familiar form which included the words, "We praise You, we adore You . . ." when he stopped short.

"No I don't," he said with the frankness which the group had long since achieved with one another. "I don't know what it means to adore God."

He knew what it was, certainly, to thank Him for specific things. And he'd often experienced exaltation when he listened to beautiful organ music during a service or saw a lovely piece of stained glass. But praise of God in and of Himself—not apropos of anything He had done, nor mediated through human skill—that, he admitted to his friends, was something he had not yet achieved.

It was not long after this that the events occurred at Yale which were so widely reported in newspapers and magazines all over the country. Many in the YCF and others on the Yale campus received the Baptism in the Holy Spirit with the charisma, including tongues. Although the press seized on tongues as making the best story, Bob Morris and the others put very little emphasis on them in their own thinking, feeling that gifts of prophecy, healing, above all the fruit of love, which the Spirit had poured out on the group were far more important. But in Bob's personal religious life tongues filled a very special gap.

"For me," Bob told us, "the gift of tongues turned out to be the gift of praise. As I used the unknown language which God had given me I felt rising in me the love, the awe, the adoration pure and uncontingent, that I had not been able to achieve in thought-out prayer. Praise and adoration are basically non-conceptual things, and glossalalia is non-conceptual prayer. It releases us from our dependence on specifics and step-by-step thought processes into a direct awareness of God —just as we're aware of the impact of a human personality without enumerating the details which go to make it up."

Nor did this new dimension in prayer hold true only when Bob was praying in tongues. He noticed at once a new ability to praise and magnify God in English. Often he would begin his devotions with tongues, feel the swelling of this new capacity in him, and then switch to English, finding his total prayer life transformed.

"I have noticed a new ability to give praise to the God revealed in Christ," he wrote for *Trinity* magazine in the flurry of national interest that followed the events at Yale. "Not just intellectual thanksgiving—but praise which seems to flow out of unknown depths in a non-emotional but fully self-filling way."

And then he adds something else. "I have also sensed very definitely a literal physical power and resiliency to meet the tasks of daily life." [2]

This added physical strength and resiliency was another purpose of tongues noted by St. Paul. The man who speaks in tongues, Paul wrote, edifies himself, or builds himself up. [3]

We have a friend who used to commute by ferry between Staten Island and Manhattan, in New York City. The trip took nearly half an hour and could have been a frustration in a busy day. But this man, David Wilkerson, used the time on the boat for prayer in tongues. He would start off by thinking of all the things he had to be thankful for. In a reversal of Bob Morris' sequence, he would review them one by one in his mind, in English, praising God for each one.

Bit by bit, inside him, he would feel a mounting sense of joy. He was conscious of being loved, taken care of. He began to glimpse pattern and design in all that was happening to him. And suddenly in trying to express his gratitude he would reach a language barrier. English could no longer express what he felt. It was simply inadequate for the Being that he perceived. It was at this point that he would burst through into communication which was not limited by vocabulary. His spirit as well as his mind would start to praise God.

Inevitably, by the time David reached the Manhattan pier a transformation had taken place. He was built up in body and in spirit. He felt emboldened, ready to tackle impossible tasks, invigorated and refreshed, ready to meet whatever the day had to offer. And this was often important, for David Wilkerson is a youth worker among street gangs in the New York slums—a job that brings him into contact with teen-age dope addicts, child prostitutes, young killers, and some of the most discouraging and intractable problems in the world today.

Here were some similar answers to my question about the value of tongues:

■"What's the *use* of speaking in tongues? The only way I can answer that is to say, 'What's the use of a bluebird? What is the use of a sunset?' Just sheer, unmitigated uplift, just joy unspeakable and with it health and peace and rest and release from burdens and tensions." Marianne Brown, housewife, Parkesburg, Pennsylvania.

■"Oftentimes—very often in fact—I have to get my night's sleep sitting up in a Greyhound bus or on a jet plane. I don't recommend it as a substitute for a good mattress. But I have a secret: the minute I close my eyes I begin to pray in the Spirit. I pray all night that way, waking up and drifting back to sleep, always praying. I don't get much sleep, but I get a lot of rest. The next morning I'm fresh and strong and ready for a full day's work." David du Plessis, Pentecostal minister, Oakland, California.

■"When I started praying in tongues I felt, and people told me I looked, twenty years younger. My conscious mind does not know what I am saying, but my unconscious and subconscious undoubtedly does, for the thing that happens is just what St. Paul said would happen, 'he who prays in an unknown tongue edifies himself.' I am built up, am given joy, courage, peace, the sense of God's Presence; and I happen to be a weak personality who needs this." William T. Sherwood, seventy-five-year-old Episcopal priest, St. Petersburg, Florida. When the Reverend Sherwood's retirement age came up, ten years ago, he wrote, he was glad: for years he'd felt underpar physically, continually tired, drained of energy. Since then he has had the Baptism in the Holy Spirit, and the most productive work-years of his life.

Another use of tongues suggested in the Bible is to let us pray even when with our own minds we have no idea what to ask for in a given situation.[4]

Lydia Maxam evidently relied heavily on this kind of prayer-in-tongues when she interceded for another person, realizing how little of his situation she could ever really know. Did other people, I wonder, use tongues this way?

Here is part of a letter I received from a psychiatrist:

Each morning before the day's appointments begin [the doctor wrote], my wife and I have a prayer time together. We pray for our own needs and then for each patient I will see that day.... We mention first our own insights into his problem, using the notes I've made during his sessions, and what we know of medicine and psychiatry. But then, realizing how much of mental illness still defies understanding, we include a prayer for him in tongues. I am frequently astonished at the healing power which is present in sessions following these prayers.

One of the most startling instances I know of when the intellect simply refused to pray in an emergency, was related to me by William C. Nelson. The Reverend Mr. Nelson is now editor of *Frontiers* for the American Baptist Convention, but at the time this incident took place was pastor of the First Baptist Church in Whitman, Massachusetts.

In the dead of night, one evening in the fall of 1959, the telephone beside Bill's bed rang. Fumbling for the receiver, Bill was still groggy when a woman's voice identified itself as belonging to a nurse at a nearby hospital. There had been an automobile accident, the voice continued.

"We have Carol Vinall here. Her mother gave your name as minister. You better get here right away if you're coming. Doctor doesn't think she'll live another hour."

"I'll be there."

Bill threw his clothes on and crowded the speed limit every mile of the way in to the hospital. The desk had been alerted that he was coming, and sent him up to the third floor. The clock across from the elevator said 3:15 A.M.

"This way," said a nurse.

Thirteen-year-old Carol lay in a high-sided bed with no sign of life about her. Her mother stood beside the oxygen tent. "It was a head-on collision," she said to Bill. "She hasn't moved since I got here." Apparently Carol had been thrown through a windshield. A doctor explained that there was injury to the brain shelf.

"If she lives," said Mrs. Vinall, "they say she might not be . . . normal."

Bill knew that he ought to pray. He was their minister. Mrs. Vinall had a right to expect support and comfort from him. But what should he pray?

He looked at Carol and felt that the doctors' guess of an hour was overlong. The girl still had her clothes on; her black sweater was torn and stained. Her hair, pulled back from her torn and bruised face, was matted with blood. The emergency stitches holding the cuts together were swollen and angry.

And the worst of the injuries, he knew, he could not see at all. Deep inside her skull the bone shelf which supported her brain was fractured. What damage was there to the brain itself? Did he have any right to pray for a physical recovery when there was every chance Carol would become a creature more like a vegetable than like a human? Yet, surely, he could not pray that she die.

Bill approached the girl and placed his hands on the one portion of her body which seemed unhurt, her right arm. Human, negative thoughts crowded in on him. "Lord," he said, "help me to know how to pray."

And right away a verse of scripture popped into Bill's mind. "We do not even know how we ought to pray, but through our inarticulate groans the Spirit himself is pleading for us, and God who searches our inmost being knows what the Spirit means. . . ." [5]

How perfectly the verses fit! Bill took a deep breath and began to pray not with his mind but with his lips and tongue only, by-passing all the doubts and hesitations of his humanity, using the sounds which God gave him. He turned the prayer over entirely to the Holy Spirit, knowing that He loved Carol more than any human could. Bill sensed a strange paradox in the situation: to the degree that he could become passive and yielding, that was the degree to which he could become an effective channel for God.

Bill prayed with the Spirit this way, quietly and under his breath, for fifteen or twenty minutes. He was only vaguely aware of the room around him: of the standing lamp which threw its beam against the wall, of the bottles of saline solution, the oxygen tent, the jars of plasma standing near Carol's bed, of the other patient in the room who was looking on in wide-eyed silence. He was conscious of Mrs. Vinall's unstirring vigil. But he was aware above all of two things that were happening inside himself. He felt a current of warmth flow through him to the little girl whose arm he held lightly in prayer. And he was aware of the strange, brilliant certainty growing stronger each moment: the sure knowledge that Carol was going to be well again.

And then Carol moved.

That was all. Just one fleeting movement. A whisper of life that touched her small body and then was gone. But it gave Bill Nelson the courage to say the thing which was singing in his heart. The thing that he was sure of. The thing that he knew!

"Mrs. Vinall, Carol is going to be all right."

Once he had spoken the words they sounded preposterous. How dare he! A nurse bent over the bed, imperturbably carrying out the schedule of respiration and plasma feedings.

The clock on the wall in the corridor said 3:45. Bill had been there just half an hour: it seemed like so much longer. Mrs. Vinall walked with him to the elevator, as though she wanted to stay close to the only voice of hope she had heard. At the elevator he told her again what he did not understand: Carol was going to get well.

And Bill was right.

Twelve weeks later, Carol was back in school. Today, five years after the accident, the only after-effects are some hairfine scars on Carol's face and arms. It is as true today, Bill Nelson believes, as it was when Paul wrote to the Romans, that when we do not know how to pray, "the Spirit comes to the aid of our weakness."

The fourth and final claim made in the Bible for tongues was that—together with the companion gift of interpretation—it provided a means for God to communicate directly with a group of Christians assembled together in worship.

I will be frank to say that as far as modern-day applications of the gift went, it was this use of tongues in public worship that alone struck me as suspect. I had by this time attended a great many Pentecostal services, and made notes on them.

"It disturbs me," I had written after one such service, "that these people have to talk so loud and use such a monotone when they speak in tongues or give an interpretation. They seem almost to go into a trance, which may mean that they're genuinely possessed by the Spirit, and may mean that they just hope to look that way." On another evening I'd written simply, "Very theatrical."

I noted that there was often no correlation between the length of the message in tongues, and the length of the interpretation. I frequently had the feeling that an interpretation (often supplied by the minister) was produced just because Paul insisted on it, and not in response to a genuine inner urging. I was usually disappointed in the content of the interpretation: more often than not it was a stereotyped exhortation to "... stand fast in the latter day...." "... walk in the way ... walk in the way of the Lord...." I was bothered, too, that the language used was almost exclusively King James English. Why should God, if He were really using this means to communicate with people here and now, not use the language of here and now?

And then, one afternoon I had a personal experience with this kind of message-from-God which from then on also had to be included in any thinking I did about it. Tib and I had gone down to Philadelphia to a meeting of "The Saturday Group"—a fluid and deliberately non-organized collection of tongues-speaking Christians, mostly from denominational churches, who took a room in the Benjamin Franklin Hotel one Saturday a month for a day-long Spirit-filled prayer meeting.

The week before we went down I had made a decision that had been bothering me ever since. It involved a young man whom I had met some years earlier in connection with a magazine story. In doing research for the article on juvenile delinquency I had happened to play a role in getting him and some others a suspended sentence on a charge of stealing. I'd been in touch with his family off and on since this time, had helped him get a job and twice been called into conference when he'd been accused of stealing on the job. Now he was in jail again, on uncontrovertible evidence and I had come to the difficult conclusion that trying to get him off, interceding in his behalf, stepping between him and the consequences had never been in his real interests.

It was a long, complex affair, involving a church group and other people, but basically the decision had been my own, and I wavered between deep conviction about it and deep doubt. Members of the boy's family had written, accusing me of being a fair-weather friend and other hard-to-deny adjectives.

At any rate, it was that weekend that we went to Philadelphia. For the first hour or so after we joined the group in their eleventh floor suite, the meeting was similar to others we had attended. There was a good deal of prayer in tongues, but it was a private prayer: either individuals worshipping quietly by themselves, or little groups of three and four "ministering" to one another.

All at once, though, a woman Methodist minister stepped to the center of the room and gave an utterance in tongues that was clearly intended for the entire group to hear. There was immediate silence. Then a man's voice interpreted. I could not see him from where I was sitting, but there was no suggestion of trance in his tone. The language used was simple, modern English, quietly spoken:

"Do not worry. I am pleased with the stand you have taken. This is difficult for you but will bring much blessing to another."

These words hit me with a power that is indescribable. I *knew* they were meant for me, specifically for me, right now. Indeed, they gave me the courage to stand by my decision in the weeks that followed even in the face of a great deal of pressure. Events have since proved that this was indeed the right tack to take with this particular problem. But what was germane to the question I had asked about tongues was the emotion of absolute certainty that was my interior reaction to that message and its interpretation. I no more questioned, at the time, that those were God's words to me, than I question the fact that there is a typewriter in front of me now.

Later, of course, I toyed with all kinds of other meanings the words could have had. But I couldn't argue away the fact of my feelings at the time. Here was something I had not read in Paul's letters and could not have guessed: that God might accompany the messages with a corroborating conviction in the hearer.

I didn't try very hard to argue it away, naturally: a message of your own from God is a wonderful thing. But it was getting a little close for comfort. When I'd set out to discover whether tongues had practical value I meant, of course, value for other people.

Chapter Nine

# Detective Story

One of the most delightful people I know is an enormously stout, jovial Jew named Jacob Rabinowitz. Tib and I were having a sandwich with him one day at a rear table in a New York delicatessen when he said quite unexpectedly:

"You've heard of an Orthodox Jew? And a Reform Jew?" We nodded. "But have you ever heard of a Completed Jew?"

When we said we had not Jacob told us his own story. He was a rabbi, the son of a rabbi, the grandson of a rabbi and so on back seventeen generations: for hundreds of years the Rabinowitzes had been rabbis of their faith. When Jacob, some years earlier, had begun to be persuaded of the truth of Christianity, he felt like a traitor to this long heritage. "I was about to become a converted Jew," he told us. "How terrible that sounds, like someone who has turned his back on his Jewishness. But I was proud to be a Jew. And today I know there's no conflict. I'm not a converted Jew, I'm a *completed* Jew, like Peter and like Paul."

And then Jacob told us about the event which left him feeling that at last he had been completed. Jacob had been, as he said, a Christian by conviction, but a guilty one—conscious of a deep split within himself. Then one sweltering summer night in July of 1960, he was invited by a friend to visit the First Assembly of God Church in Pasadena, Texas, where a revival was in progress. A little reluctantly, because he was wary of emotionalism, Jacob agreed to go.

The service was typically Pentecostal. There were songs and testimonies and hand-clapping and at last a sermon. At the end of his address, the revivalist invited anyone present who had a personal problem to come forward to the altar rail and receive the prayers of the congregation.

Suddenly Jacob was seized with a great longing to lay down the burdensome double life he had carried so long, to resolve once and for all the conflict within him. He went forward and knelt with some others at the railing. But when the preacher asked him what his special need was, Jacob remained silent.

"That's all right," the revival leader said. "God knows what your needs are better than you know yourself." And turning to the congregation he requested prayer "in the Spirit" for Jacob.

Several men at once left their seats and came to stand around the kneeling rabbi. Some stood beside, some behind him; a few laid their hands on his head and shoulders, others simply bowed their heads. Then they began to pray, speaking simultaneously, some in English, others in tongues.

Suddenly Jacob raised his head and turned to look behind him. His cheeks were flushed and tear-wet.

"That was beautiful," he said. "Which one of you is Jewish?"

No one answered.

"Which one of you knows me? You'll forgive me: I don't recognize you. . . ."

Still no answer.

Now the whole church became silent. "It came from right here, behind me," said Jacob. "Just exactly where you're standing," he said to one of the men. "Are you Jewish?"

"Me?" The man smiled. "My name's John Gruver. I'm Irish."

"That's the voice! That's the voice!" said the rabbi, excited now. "But you . . . you do speak Hebrew?"

"Not a word of it," said Gruver.

Jacob stood up. "That's where you're wrong," he said. "Because you were speaking Hebrew just now. . . ."

As Jacob told us the story, his voice filled with emotion. "Can you imagine that great big Irishman behind me speaking the most beautiful Hebrew I ever heard? Can you imagine an Irishman speaking Hebrew at all?"

"And how did he know my father's name? No one in Texas knew my family. But here's what he said. 'I have dreamed a dream'—in Hebrew he said it, perfect Hebrew—'I have dreamed a dream that you will go into the big populated places and there you will preach. The ones who have not heard will understand you because you, Jacob, son of Rabbi Ezekiel, come in the fullness of the blessing of the Gospel of Jesus Christ.' "

The rabbi looked at us. "What do you make of that!" He took his napkin out of his collar and shoved back his chair. "God was speaking to me as a Jew and as a Christian too. There was no difference. In Jesus Christ every difference is swallowed up."

That settled it for me.

For months I'd been trying to avoid an obvious discrepancy in stories about tongues. In one kind of account the tongue is never recognized by either speaker or hearers but remains to the end a collection of meaningless sound. This was obviously the kind of tongue St. Paul was familiar with. "For one who speaks in a tongue speaks not to men . . . for no one understands him. . . ." [1] "Unknown tongues" was the name often given in the Bible to this phenomenon, and is still the kind most frequently encountered today.

On the other hand there have been instances both in Bible times and since when a tongue that is meaningless to the speaker has been recognized by someone else, and where the fact of its being a known language has been an essential part of its effectiveness. Pentecost itself as recorded in the book of Acts is an example. Street throngs in Jerusalem were impressed by Jesus' adherents *because* they heard them speaking real languages that they couldn't have known by natural means. To Pachomius a mystic knowledge of Greek must have been of great value in his dealings with strangers with whom this was the only common language. The Jew who wandered into the Azusa Street meetings was converted *because* Kathleen Scott spoke to him in Hebrew.

I knew I could no longer ignore these stories. They were cropping up too often among people we knew personally. Harald Bredesen said that he'd spoken in Polish and in Arabic both, Jacob Rabinowitz heard an Irishman speak Hebrew, and just that week I'd had a letter from Dennis Bennett— written from Seattle in excellent typing, from which I perceived that the little mission church now had a secretary— saying that a truck driver in his parish had received the Baptism and that his tongue had been recognized by a Chinaman as Mandarin Chinese.

"Do you believe these stories?" I asked Tib as we drove home from our lunch with Jacob.

She thought about it a moment. "I believe the people who tell the stories," she said.

I knew what she meant. It was impossible to think of Harald and Jacob and Dennis as deliberately lying to persuade me of something, since they so obviously believed what they said themselves. Their lives had been reshaped by these experiences: they would hardly be acting out elaborate, lifelong deceptions.

Patently, what they both claimed and believed in were miracles. But here I balked. Surely there were natural, non-miraculous explanations for these things. I went through my correspondence with tongues-speakers, lifting out every letter which purported to record an instance of the Spirit's putting a known language on someone's lips. I stacked them on my desk and they made an impressive pile. The job I now set myself was to find an explanation for each one which satisfied both logic and the facts the writer supplied.

Wasn't it possible, for instance, that these "miracles" were nothing more than a trick of the subconscious memory? The speaker had heard the language long ago, perhaps as a child, and retained phrases in his subconscious while forgetting with his conscious mind any contact with it.

At first I thought I was on a trail that was leading somewhere. Because in many letters I did find words like "snatches of" or "phrases from" or "words that sounded like" known languages. These, it seemed to me, were easy to explain on the forgotten-exposure basis.

Harder to account for on this theory were instances where someone spoke not a phrase or two in a foreign language but carried on a long, connected discourse. Mr. Roy H. Wead, of South Bend, Indiana, had written me this account of an event that occurred in 1934. The "Brother Richardson" in the story is Mr. L. B. Richardson, today of Jacksonville, Florida, but who in 1934 was attending the same Pentecostal Bible school as Roy Wead.

...Brother Richardson, at the time [writes Mr. Wead], was going through a great testing, with considerable doubts relative to the Baptism of the Holy Spirit. He had doubts even about his own experience, when he received the Holy Spirit as a child some years earlier.

He began to seek the Lord in his room in school and continued there praying most of the day. My room being across the hall, I could hear him pray as I went to classes. In the afternoon, after some hours of prayer, it was evident that he had gone through to a wonderful victory and was rejoicing in the Lord, praising and worshipping the Lord in unknown tongues as moved by the Spirit.

Still later, as I came down the hall to my room, I noted a young Chinaman, Samuel Ko, who was attending the school, standing there in the hall next to Brother Richardson's room, listening to him speak in unknown tongues. Brother Ko, very elated, began to tell me that Brother Richardson was speaking in Chinese and that he, Brother Ko, could understand what he was saying. He further stated that Brother Richardson was speaking about things in China which Brother Ko was familiar with. Brother Richardson had been speaking in Chinese for some minutes: at least half an hour, or considerably longer.

The letter went on to say that Richardson had no knowledge of ever having been exposed to Chinese. The experience greatly encouraged him: his period of testing was over.

"All right," I said to myself. "Supposing always for the sake of this inquiry that Mr. Wead is both honest and has a pretty good memory—Richardson spoke Chinese for half an hour. Isn't it conceivable that in some harder-to-imagine but not impossible way, Richardson not only heard Chinese as a very small child, too young to remember it, but had been fluent in it?"

Suppose he'd had a little Chinese playmate or a Chinese nursemaid who talked aloud about the things in China that Ko recognized. We know that Richardson was in a very emotional state when this happened; he'd been praying for many hours—wasn't this precisely when some such long-buried material might be jarred out of hiding?

A more telling rebuttal would be if a child, whose whole exposure-history was known, should speak a real foreign language—and among Pentecostals it is very common for children to speak in tongues. In fact I soon found an account of just such an event among the heap of letters on my desk. This one was from William C. Pickthorn, Palo Alto, California.

He was relating events which he had recorded in his diary on Saturday, July 30, 1932.

This story occurred at a cottage prayer meeting which, according to my diary, was held "about two miles from the Noy Mine" out of Ironwood, Michigan. I was helping a pastor by the name of Block who was trying to establish a church in Ironwood. Rev. Block was pastor of Winegar, Wisconsin. He had witnessed to a great number of people in surrounding towns and then he had called the evangelistic team of which I was a member to try to capitalize this witnessing into an organized body of believers.

Public meetings were held in a tent in Ironwood. Quite a number of responsible people who were well known in the community came to the service. The diary entry of July 30th, records a visit in the home of a family named Erickson. A young lady who had spoken to me the night before was there. Her mother had been healed by the Rev. Block the previous winter through prayer. The whole family had been interested in the Baptism of the Spirit, but were afraid of the experience because they were told "tongues" was of the devil. The mother said she would like to attend one of the cottage meetings, but was afraid to do so.

She finally agreed, and was present. I noted particularly that she was watching a boy of about 12 years of age, who sat on the floor with his hands clasped about his knees. The boy was praying fervently. While I watched, he began to speak in a language which I could not understand. Then he began to sing in a language which I did not understand.

Mrs. Erickson began to cry. I was quite disturbed, and tried to apologize to her. Her reply to me was somewhat as follows: "No, this boy has not upset me. That is not why I was crying. I have known this boy all his life. I was with his mother when he was born. He has just sung a song to me in praise of God, a song I never heard before and a song I know he has never heard before, and he spoke it in my language, Swedish, and he does not know my language. When he was praying, he was praying in Swedish."

If this information was complete, it certainly argued against the subconscious-memory theory. But was it complete? Mrs.

Erickson could not have been with the boy every minute of his twelve years, however well she believed she knew him. And he was living in a part of the world where Swedish immigrants had settled in great numbers.

Then I ran across a story which I could fit in no way into my forgotten-exposure hypothesis.

One day a young man from New Jersey, Clifford Tonnensen, had attended a Pentecostal camp meeting in Michigan. In the course of the meeting Clifford received the Baptism in the Holy Spirit and began to speak in tongues.

A lady standing nearby grew extremely excited. Clifford was speaking German, she said. A fluent, beautiful High German.

But this alone was not what excited the lady. It was the fact that she *knew* he could not be speaking the language by any natural means. He could not even speak his own language, English. Clifford was a deaf-mute who had not heard a sound since a disease destroyed his hearing at the age of two months!

Coupled with accounts like this, I now admitted, was another factor which argued against memory as the source of some of these seeming miracles. Sometimes the speaker, in the course of exercising the foreign tongue, mentioned facts or events which only the hearer knew. John Gruver spoke of Jacob Rabinowitz' father by name. Kathleen Scott told the visitor to Azusa Street why he had come to Los Angeles and what his occupation was. Even if these people had come naturally by the language, how had they come to the facts?

I pushed my chair back, put my feet up, and reviewed the state of my investigation. No doubt some cases of tricks-of-memory may have existed, but I was becoming certain that there were many accounts which could not be explained in this way. "I've got to try another tack," I said to the filing cabinet.

And this time I turned my attention to the Bible. There is

only one instance in Scripture of tongues being recognized as known languages, and this is at Pentecost itself. I read through the event again.

And as I did three verses leapt out at me. They each repeated the same idea: once, twice, a third time.

The sentence preceding this thrice-expressed idea was the one I was by now so familiar with: "And they were all filled with the Holy Ghost, and began to speak with other tongues, as the Spirit gave them utterance." But then there followed these verses:

Now when this was noised abroad, the multitude came together, and were confounded, because that every man heard them speak in his own language.

And they were all amazed and marvelled, saying one to another, Behold, are not all these which speak Galilaeans? And how hear we every man in our own tongue, wherein we were born? ...

... we do hear them speak in our tongues the wonderful works of God.[2]

Didn't this suggest that the focus of attention should be not on the speaker, but on the hearer? In the crowd "every man *heard* them speak in his own language." And as if to hammer home the point, "How *hear* we every man in our own tongue," and "... we do *hear* them speak in our tongues...."

Could it be that the miracle was not so much a phenomenon of the lips as of the ears? A lot would suddenly fall into place with this interpretation.

It would explain, for instance, how L. B. Richardson could have been heard speaking for half an hour in Chinese. Nonsense syllables were imbued with meaning by Samuel Ko's eager hearing. Like the listeners at Pentecost: he heard Richardson speak in his own language.

It would explain how a young child whose language-contacts were known could have been heard by Mrs. Erickson to speak Swedish. And how a deaf boy, who could not even speak his own language, could have been heard speaking German. It would even explain all those cases where the message of the tongue contained allusions known only to the hearer.

But it could not adequately explain instances where not one but several people heard the same thing. To account for this as a phenomenon-of-hearing I would have to believe that the identical interior process had worked simultaneously in each listener's head, which would be a miracle in itself.

Dr. T. J. McCrossan of Minneapolis tells the story of nine U.S. Marines who, one Saturday night, entered a small Pentecostal church in Seattle, Washington, drawn by the music, and then listened in growing amazement as an American woman whom they knew arose and gave a message in tongues. All nine of the Marines were Filipinos, all nine recognized an obscure Filipino dialect and agreed on the sense of what they'd heard. The woman, they knew, could not naturally speak Filipino at all, much less this strange dialect from a region rarely visited by Westerners.

A somewhat similar experience took place on Easter Sunday, 1950, in a small Pentecostal church in Gary, Indiana. A member of the congregation, Paul Goodwin, stood up and delivered an exhortation in tongues. As he spoke there was an agitated stirring among a group of Italians in the congregation, and when he finished a young man named Leo Pella got up and said:

"We know Paul Goodwin, and he does not speak our language. But he has just spoken in perfect Italian, as though he had graduated from a college in Italy."

But the most amazing story in my collection concerned a group of people who recognized their own language not on foreign soil but at home; the speaker in this case was the foreigner. It was an adventure which took place in the heart of Africa in the year 1922.

In that year, the Reverend H. B. Garlock and his wife, of Toms River, New Jersey, volunteered for a dangerous assignment: they were to go to Africa as missionaries to the Pahns, a small tribe in the interior of Liberia. No missionaries had ever before worked with the Pahns. The reason was simple. The Pahns were cannibals.

The Garlocks arrived in Liberia and set up camp with a group of African Christians whose tribal boundary touched that of the Pahns. Almost immediately Mrs. Garlock came down with malaria. Their meager medical chest was soon emptied and still her fever rose. Garlock had a difficult time persuading the natives to take a short route to the coast for more medicine because the way led through Pahn country.

At last, however, Garlock convinced the chief that it was possible to skirt the danger areas, and that if medicine didn't arrive soon, Mrs. Garlock might well die. One morning at dawn a group of men left the compound and headed out, filled with misgivings, to bring back supplies.

About noon the head carrier suddenly appeared in the doorway of the mud hut where Mrs. Garlock lay. He was out of breath. In gasps he blurted out what had happened. One of his men had been captured by the cannibals. The African assured the two missionaries that unless the man could be rescued, he would be eaten.

Garlock realized that it was his fault. Providentially, his wife's fever had begun to go down that very morning, within an hour after the supply party had left. Without hesitation Garlock himself set out into Pahn territory, taking along a few hand-picked warriors: he was going to try to get the man out.

Just before dark, the little group arrived at the village where the carrier was being held. A wooden fence ran around the cluster of huts, but no one stood guard. Garlock peeked cautiously through and saw that one of the huts had sentries posted before it. Two men carrying spears squatted outside in the dust. Their hair was braided in long pigtails; their front teeth were filed to a point.

That would be the prison, Garlock decided. He turned to his men. "I'm going in," he whispered. "If there's trouble, make as much noise as you can. I'll try to get away in the confusion."

Garlock was counting on two facts to help him. One was the probability that the Pahns had never seen a white man: he hoped that this would give him the advantage of surprise. The other was that he believed the miracle stories of the Bible, telling of supernatural help coming when it was needed most. Garlock was praying as he stepped into the cannibals' compound. He was praying that God would show him step by step what he should do.

Walking as straight and as tall as he could, he strode directly toward the prison hut. The guards were too astonished to stop him. He walked between them and ducked inside the hut. Outside, he heard the guards begin to shout: he heard feet slap against the packed earth as others ran to join them. In the dark interior Garlock crawled forward until his hands touched a figure tied to the center pole of the hut.

Garlock slipped a knife out of his pocket and cut the bonds. The carrier spoke to him, but seemed incapable of making any effort in his own behalf. Garlock dragged the terrified man out through the door. But that's as far as he got. There in the courtyard was a yelling, threatening crowd of Africans armed with knives, spears and hatchets.

Garlock listened for his own men to start a distraction. But outside the compound all was silence. Garlock knew that he had been abandoned.

There was nothing for it except to try a bluff. With great deliberation he settled the prisoner up against the hut, and then he himself sat down on the skull of an elephant that stood beside the door. All the while he was praying. The crowd kept its distance, still yelling and milling, but not coming close.

A full moon rose. Garlock sat quietly on his elephant's skull. Finally the people squatted down in a great semi-circle facing the hut. In the center of this ring, Garlock thought he spotted the chief and beside him the village witch doctor.

Suddenly this man stood up. He ran a few steps toward Garlock, then stopped. He held out a reed wand, shook it at Garlock, then started to stalk back and forth between the missionary and the chief, talking loudly and gesturing occasionally toward the prisoner. Garlock could not understand a word he said, but it was clear to him that he was on trial.

The witch doctor harrangued Garlock for an hour, and then quite abruptly he stopped. He came, for the first time, directly up to Garlock and peered into his face. The witch doctor thrust his neck forward, then drew it back amid the cheers of the onlookers. Then, with great ostentation, he laid the wand on the ground at Garlock's feet. He stepped back, waiting.

Silence fell over the tribe. Garlock gathered that it was now time for him to speak in his own defense.

But how! Garlock did not know one word of the Pahn language. The crowd began to grow restless. Stalling for time Garlock stood up and picked up the wand. Instantly the natives fell silent. And while they waited, Garlock prayed.

"Lord, show me what to do. Send your Spirit to help me."

Suddenly Garlock began to shake violently. This frightened him as he did not want the others to see that he was afraid. But with the trembling came a sense of the nearness of the Holy Spirit. Words of Jesus came to him: "Take no thought what ye shall speak, neither do ye premeditate; but whatsoever shall be given to you in that hour, that speak ye; for it is not ye that speak but the Holy Ghost." [3]

Garlock felt a strange boldness. He took a deep breath and

began to speak. From his lips came a flow of words which he did not understand.

Garlock saw the natives lean forward, enthralled. He saw that the words—whatever they were—had a stirring effect on those who listened. He knew beyond a doubt that he was speaking to the Pahns in their own language.

For twenty minutes Garlock talked to the Pahns. Then, as suddenly as the speech-power came, it vanished, and Garlock knew that he had come to the end of his discourse. He sat down.

There was a moment of waiting while the chief and the witch doctor put their heads together. Then, straightening, the witch doctor gave an order and a white rooster was brought forward. With a snap, the witch doctor wrung the rooster's neck. He sprinkled some of the blood on the foreheads of Garlock and the prisoner. Later Garlock interpreted this as meaning that the rooster had taken his place: blood had to be shed, but something he had said while speaking in the Spirit had convinced these people that he and the prisoner should go free.

A few minutes later, Garlock and the captured man were walking through the jungle back toward the mission station. The chief had even supplied two of his own men to guide them the first part of the journey. In time, the Pahns gave up their cannibal life and were converted to Christianity. Garlock is certain that the beginnings of the conversion came with the seed sown while he stood in a flood of moonlight and gave a speech, not one word of which did he understand.

I had come to a pause in my work, and I tried to look objectively at the state of my research. Was I really any closer than before to knowing whether real language was spoken? There were plenty of case histories available which suggested various answers, but wasn't there an inherent flaw in the case history approach itself?

What, I asked myself, was the source of all these stories? I had gathered them from letters written to me by people who spoke in tongues, and from articles published by people who spoke in tongues, and from interviews with people who spoke in tongues. In other words, I was depending on prejudiced witnesses. Of necessity, all the stories I had collected came from people who were not objective observers, but just the opposite: they were deeply involved participants with something personal at stake in the conclusions.

For months I had been making tape recordings of people speaking in tongues. If I should play these before a group of disinterested language experts and one of *them* should recognize a language, the position would be different. I could make a study of linguistic background of the speaker, feeling that the inquiry was based on something solid.

About three weeks later, I met with David Scott, religious book editor at McGraw-Hill, and six linguists, in a private dining room at the Columbia University Faculty Club. Three of the linguists were on the staff at Columbia, two were professors at Union Theological Seminary, and one at General Theological Seminary. There were two specialists in modern languages, three in ancient languages, and one expert in the study of language structure.

I was interested in their reactions to our experiment. They were extremely attentive, dubious without being hostile. As I put on the first tape, each man leaned forward, straining to catch every syllable. Several took notes. But at no time did I see a face light up with recognition. I played another tape, and then another. For the better part of an hour we listened to one prayer after another, spoken "in the Spirit." And when, at last, we came to the end, I looked around and asked,

"Well, Gentlemen?"

Six heads shook in the negative.

Not one had heard a language which he could identify.

Yet there were some interesting observations along the way.

One of the linguists reported that although he did not identify words he felt that one tape had been structured in much the same way a modern poem is structured. "Modern poetry depends upon sound as much as upon verbal meaning to get across its message," he said. "In this one prayer, I felt that although I didn't understand the literal sense of her words, I did catch the emotional content of what she was saying. It was a hymn of love. Beautiful."

It was interesting, too, that although no language known to these men was recorded, they had frequently identified language *patterns* on the tapes. The "shape" of real language, the variety of sound combinations, infrequency of repetition and so forth, is virtually impossible, so they said, to reproduce by deliberate effort. Remembering Dina Donohue's parody of tongues-speaking, I had slipped onto the tapes two instances of pure made-up gibberish, one by our son, Scott, and one by Tib. They had tried to sound as much as possible like the tongues on the rest of the tape, but the linguists spotted the deception immediately.

"That's not language," one man said. "That's just noise."

As they rose to leave another of the professors made the point that according to the last census taken by the French Academy there are nearly 2800 known languages and dialects currently spoken in the world today—without taking into account all the languages that have appeared on earth and then vanished. "And the Academy called even the list of current languages far from complete," he said. "Among us, here in this room, we speak only a tiny fraction of these. Even if there were real language on those tapes, the odds against our recognizing it are enormous."

Although we did not say so to these scholars, we knew that from the Pentecostal's viewpoint the current and obsolete languages of earth were only the beginning. Operating in a world beyond the mortal, the Pentecostal believes his tongue may have its origin in spiritual spheres. I had always read the opening words of St. Paul's great thirteenth chapter of First Corinthians, "Though I speak with the tongues of men and of angels," in a poetic sense. But seen in the context of the chapters before and after, there is no doubt in my mind now that Paul was speaking of tongues in the specific Pentecostal sense, and of angel tongues as one variety of these.

The net results of the experiment, however, were negative. We had taken some forty examples of tongues to language experts and not one had turned out to be recognizable. My attempt to discover whether real language was or was not spoken did not seem to have led me to a crisp conclusion, so I decided to turn my attention into different channels.

Strangely, the strongest argument in favor of doing so came from the people who spoke in tongues. One day I was talking with Dr. Howard Ervin a Baptist minister in Atlantic Highlands, New Jersey, and a strong believer in the value of tongues, about my attempt to isolate language in them.

"Are you sure you're not making a basic mistake?" asked Dr. Ervin.

"I must be: I'm not coming up with answers."

"I think the mistake is to divorce tongues from the essential whole of which they're a part," said Dr. Ervin. "Let me tell you a little story. I happen to be fond of church architecture. One day when I was out driving I found an exquisite little Gothic chapel. I stopped my car and got out to admire it.

"But that little church happened to have at its entrance a bright, red door. My eyes would try to follow the soaring lines of the building upward as Gothic architecture makes you do, but every time they were jerked back to that red door. It was so flamboyant it kept me from seeing the whole picture.

"Tongues, John, are like that door. As long as you stand outside your attention is going to be riveted there and you're not going to be able to see anything else. Once you go through, however, you are surrounded by the thousand wonders of light and sound and form that the architect intended. You look around and that door isn't even red on the inside. It's there. It's to be used. But it has taken its proper place in the design of the whole Church.

"That's what I'd hope for you, John. I think it's time for you to walk through that door. If you really want to discover what the Pentecostal experience is all about, don't concentrate on tongues, but step through the door and meet the Holy Spirit."

Chapter Ten

# The Baptism in the Holy Spirit

I told a friend at church next Sunday about Dr. Ervin's red door. He smiled a little wistfully. "Well, when you meet the Holy Spirit," he said, "please introduce me. I've never had a very clear idea about Him."

He wasn't the only one. I remember one Sunday when I was a small boy growing up in Louisville, Kentucky, hearing a sermon on the Holy Ghost. It was the one and only time I heard Him mentioned more than in passing from our pulpit, and all that I recall of the occasion is that my sister and I drew spook-forms down the side of the bulletin and were darkly frowned upon by an usher.

But was I really any better informed now? Wasn't the Holy Ghost still a shadow? An aspect of God, the third member of the Trinity, a concept you acknowledged every Sunday in the Creed; but a ghost just the same, as if He were the featureless remnant of someone who at one time in the Church's life had been very real indeed, but now was little more than a memory.

I knew that the personal pronoun was correct in referring to

Him; the right word was He, not It. But I didn't act as though I believed this. Near the hospital in our neighboring town of Mount Kisco there is a traffic light. If I needed to cross that street and get to the hospital in a hurry I could appeal fervently to the traffic light, but I couldn't change its pattern by a single second. I'd get across, all right; but only when the machinery inside had completed an automatic cycle. Occasionally, however, a policeman will turn off the mechanical light and direct traffic himself at that corner. If he were there when I made my urgent appeal, I would doubtless see the normal course of traffic interrupted, pattern broken, an exception made. In my prayers, when the name of the Holy Spirit was invoked at all, I noted that He filled more the function of the traffic light than the traffic officer.

Dr. Ervin had suggested that I step through the red door and meet the Holy Spirit. Before I could consider doing this, I wanted to get some more information about this Entity I was being invited to meet. So, once again armed with concordance and Bible, I set out to find it.

Some years ago I had an interview with Robert Frost. The poet drew an image which stood out with particular vividness in my mind as I set out on my search.

"If you would have out the way a man feels about God," he said, "don't ask him for a credo, but instead watch his life. It's as though a coin were hidden under a piece of paper. You can't see it directly, but you can discover the denomination by rubbing a pencil over the paper. From all the individual rises and valleys, your answer will come out."

I hoped to use this technique with the Holy Spirit. I wanted to find out who He was not by reading various credos, but by watching Him in action in the Bible. Perhaps by examining the rises and valleys I would get a portrait of Him.

I thought that references to the Spirit would be all in the New Testament, but to my surprise I found that they were not. It is true that the precise words "Holy Spirit" appear only three times in the Old Testament, but the evolving concept of the Spirit is there way back in Genesis.

One of the first things that I noticed was that the confusion as to whether the Spirit was more like an inanimate force or more like a person dates right back to the beginning of Biblical thought on the subject. The root word for "spirit" in Hebrew is "ruäh" and this word has two distinct meanings. One is "wind." And the other is "breath." One is an impersonal force, the other is much more intimate, assuming consciousness and awareness, for you cannot have breath without having someone who breathes.

The basic quality of both, however, was movement. Ruäh was always in action. It was moving. It was going to affect whatever it came in contact with.

Another concept inherent in the ancient use of the word was creativity. Ruäh was intimately associated with birth. It was the Spirit of God which moved upon the face of the water at Creation. It was the breath of life breathed into the nostrils which made man a living soul.

In later books of the Old Testament, the Spirit is depicted as playing a special role in the lives of certain individuals. The coming of the Spirit to a human being is usually accompanied by an abrupt change in personality. Samuel told Saul that the Spirit of Jehovah would come mightily upon him, and that afterwards he would be so changed as to be like another man. And indeed young Saul of "the humblest of all the families from the least of the tribes of Israel" was transformed into one of the Old Testament's great leaders.

The Spirit habitually made heroes of ordinary men. It was the Spirit of Jehovah which gave Samson his strength. The Spirit of God came upon Joshua just before he blew the trumpet that signaled the fall of Jericho. David considered that it was God's spirit which spoke through him. The list of men who were touched by the Spirit is the Old Testament's roster of giants:

| | |
|---|---|
| Joseph | Hosea |
| Moses | Amos |
| Joshua | Obadiah |
| Jephthah | Jonah |
| Nathan | Micah |
| Gad | Nahum |
| Ezekiel | Habakkuk |
| Daniel | Haggai |
| Joel | Malachi |

But there was another aspect to God's Spirit coming upon a man. In the 51st and 139th psalms the Spirit visits the poet not as a source of strength for mighty acts, but an intimate Presence, subtle by comparison, a guide not of armies, but of one man's soul:

Create in me a clean heart, O God; and renew a right spirit within me. Cast me not away from thy presence; and take not thy Holy Spirit from me.[1]

O Lord, thou hast searched me, and known me.

Thou hast beset me behind and before, and laid thine hand upon me.

Whither shall I go from thy Spirit? or whither shall I flee from thy presence?[2]

In these lines there is a sense of God's immanence quite different from the fear-filled worship of distant and unapproachable Jehovah.

The parallel to Christian thought is inescapable, and this, in fact, was the next observation I made. In those Old Testament passages which Christians believe foreshadow Christ, the Spirit figures prominently. The most striking of these prophecies come in Isaiah:

And there shall come forth a shoot out of the stock of Jesse, and a branch out of his roots shall bear fruit: and the Spirit of Jehovah shall rest upon him. . . .[3]

Behold, my servant, whom I uphold; my chosen, in whom my soul delighteth: I have put my Spirit upon him; he will bring forth justice to the Gentiles.[4]

If this were true, I should expect to find a flurry of references to the Spirit at the time of Jesus' birth. And there they were. Jesus, Himself, was conceived by the Holy Ghost. Simeon was promised by the Spirit that he would see the Messiah before he died. John the Baptist, the principal actor in the drama-of-recognition which attended Christ's coming, was associated with the Holy Spirit from the beginning. John's mother was filled with the Spirit upon being greeted by Mary. His father received the Spirit on the day the child was named. John himself was filled with the Holy Spirit from the moment of his birth. In addition, there was to be a specific sign by which John was to know the Christ when he saw Him: upon whomever he saw the Spirit descending, that person was the Son of God.

Christ's earthly ministry did not start until after the Spirit was given to Him at His baptism. It was through the Spirit's power that Jesus worked His miracles, through this power also that men were to enter the Kingdom that He preached. "Except one be born of water and the Spirit," Christ said, "he cannot enter into the kingdom of God." [5]

As His death appoached, Jesus began to prepare the disciples for the coming of this power—telling them that it was expedient for them that He should go away, for if He did not, the Spirit would not come. But when He, the Spirit, did come, He would stay with them forever. He would guide and teach and strengthen them, and in His power they would do greater works even than Christ had done.

After his death, Jesus reminded the disciples of this promise and commanded them to remain in Jerusalem until the Spirit came upon them. I paused at this point in my reading and tried to summarize what I had discovered about this Spirit who was coming:

■In the Old and New Testaments both, the Spirit is thought of in terms of action. Words that suggest movement—fire, wind, breath, rain, dove—are used to refer to Him. The Spirit is dynamic: He is God in action.

■In the Old Testament there are inferences that the Spirit is personal; in the New Testament this side of Him is stressed. Christ is constantly giving names to the Spirit which describe His shepherding, brooding, caring nature. He calls the Spirit guide, counselor, comforter, advocate.

■In both the Old and New Testaments the concept of power and Spirit are closely allied. In the Old Testament the power operates principally through great kings and prophets who lead the nation. In the New Testament the power is now about to be bestowed on the ordinary people who follow Christ.

■In both Testaments, when the Spirit touches human life, personality is transformed.

This, then, was the portrait that emerged from following the hills and valleys of the Holy Spirit's activity. The disciples waited now in Jerusalem for the arrival of this Spirit. And when, at Pentecost, He came, He transformed the timid band of disciples (literally, "learners") into apostles ("ones who are sent"). The men and women who waited in the Upper Room embarked immediately on an amazing series of power-filled acts. That very day, Peter—the same Peter who had fled for his life on the night of Jesus' arrest a few short weeks before—stood boldly up in the full hearing of the authorities and preached a sermon so eloquent and convincing that 3000 people were converted on the spot. This from a fisherman, and one from the little-regarded hinterland of Galilee at that!

It was not surprising that after this the apostles insisted that their new converts receive this power too. It was the necessary tool without which they could not carry out the tremendous task which Christ had given them.

What did it feel like, to receive the Holy Spirit? There are no full descriptions in the Bible, but from what is said we can fill in the picture.

In the first place, if the Holy Spirit is God in His dynamic aspect, knowing Him would necessarily have to be an *experience*. It would be the experience, furthermore, of a Personality, and one who deeply cared. It would be the experience of friendship. A creative, transforming friendship, in some instances fragile as a dove, in others searing as fire, like all good friendships, elusive and mysterious.

"Baptism" is just one of the words used in the Bible to describe the moment when a man comes into full contact with this friendship. The other terms, too, bolster the idea that the Holy Spirit is God in action. Sometimes, I read, the Spirit "fell" on men. Sometimes they were "filled" with the Spirit. At others they "received" the Spirit. The Spirit is said to "proceed from" God.

There was a quality about the experience that produced two responses. In first place there were tongues. And then, at Pentecost, anyway, they got a little rowdy, enough so that the people watching wondered if they were drunk. It struck me as a curious contrast with the sobersides pulpits of today that the first Christian sermon should begin with a stout denial by the preacher that he and his friends were drunk. Why, he said, it's only nine in the morning, how could anyone be drunk?

And how, in New Testament times, did people enter into this experience? There seemed to be several ways. At Pentecost the disciples simply assembled together and waited expectantly. But Cornelius and his friends and relatives, listening to Peter preach about Christ, were expecting nothing when the Spirit fell upon them. In other cases a Spirit-filled Christian passed Him to others by laying his hands upon them.

I closed the Bible, feeling that what I'd been reading had a strangely contemporary feel. I knew where the feeling came from. The letters in my file, the interviews with Spirit-filled people, all showed that little had changed in this area of the Spirit since the New Testament was written. Even the manner in which He descended on those first-century Christians had parallels today.

I remembered one recent instance where a group of people, listening to God's word as Cornelius' household was, and no more expecting the Holy Spirit than they had, were suddenly overwhelmed the same way. In 1954 a Mennonite preacher, Gerald Derstine, was conducting a week-long Bible study seminar in northern Minnesota. One day, without warning, a young man in the class suddenly knelt down and began to cry.

"This kind of emotion was very unusual in the Mennonite church," says Derstine, "and at first we tried to put a stop to it. But before we could, another student was crying. And then another. We tried to pull the weeping students out of the classroom, but as soon as we took one out two or three others began to cry.

"And then we noticed an amazing thing: strange sounds were coming from the mouths of some of these young people. Were these the 'stammering lips' we had read about in the Bible?

"Never before, to my knowledge, had such a thing happened in our church. The Mennonites do not teach that these manifestations are for today: as far as we were concerned, they belonged back nineteen hundred years ago. And yet, there before our eyes, our students were suddenly speaking in tongues, just as at Pentecost."

A friend of ours, Lila Ginter, was filled with the Spirit as a child, without even knowing that such a religious experience existed. Lila was standing in her father's apple orchard in Ohio one day, looking up through clouds of white blossoms to the blue sky overhead, when she suddenly had an overwhelming sense of the presence of God. She opened her mouth to talk to Him in the unself-conscious way of children, but the sounds which came out of her mouth were not English, and though she prattled on fluently for a long while, her lips would form no sensible words at all.

"I never told this experience to anyone," Lila told me. "I thought I was the only human being who had ever had such a thing happen. It was forty years before I discovered that there were whole groups of people to whom this phenomenon was normal."

More common, today, is for the experience to come because someone is consciously, actively seeking it. But there is as much variety in ways of seeking as there was in the Bible. Some take their cue from Christ's injunction to the disciples, "And behold I send the promise of my Father upon you: but tarry ye in the city of Jerusalem, until ye be endued with power from on high." [6] The word they stress is "tarry." They feel that they must wait, sometimes for days, praying and praising God until the Baptism comes. Others feel that there is no need to tarry. They point to other occasions in the New Testament when the Spirit was given as soon as the believer asked for Him.

Some feel that the candidate must be in a state of deep prayer before he can receive this Baptism. But others take just the opposite view: they feel that the Baptism is not a kind of Christian spectacular, but an ordinary, almost routine step in the life of a believer.

How about emotion going along with it? Some say that together with tongues should come an "interior witness": a "sense" that one's own spirit and the Holy Spirit are in communion. Others believe that the Baptism occurs on a level entirely separate from that of emotion: and is more dependable when unaccompanied by the least trace of feeling.

Absolute criteria seem to be about the only things absent from the experience of Baptism in the Holy Spirit. "And I'd worry about it if it were any other way," Tib said one night as we were discussing this. "If the Spirit is like the wind, blowing where it wants to, fixed rules would be suspicious. It'd be like coming in out of a tornado and switching on an electric fan."

But although this wind of the Spirit "bloweth where it listeth" [7] it is also undeniable that certain individuals, today as in apostolic times, have a special ministry for passing it along. In the earlier days of the Pentecostal revival, the late J. E. Stiles used to travel around the world meeting with small groups of Christians, praying for them to receive the Spirit. Literally thousands came into the experience at these meetings. David du Plessis has this special ministry. So does the Reverend Richard Winkler, rector of Trinity Episcopal Church, Wheaton, Illinois.

One of the most active people we know, in this area, is a woman. Jean Stone is a housewife and mother in suburban Van Nuys, California. She was a member of St. Mark's Episcopal Church in Van Nuys at the time of the uproar over Dennis Bennett's sermon. Jean felt that the misunderstanding never would have occurred if people had been better informed about the modern-day working of the Spirit. One evening she announced to her husband that she had decided to start a magazine which would fill this function in other parishes.

"I just smiled knowingly," said Jean's husband, Donald. "Jean didn't have the business sense to subscribe to a magazine, much less start one." Donald Stone and I were talking in a New York hotel room where he had come on a business trip.

"She was completely impractical," he went on. "She had some idea for a slick-paper, sophisticated quarterly which would be aimed at high-brows. She was going to call it *Trinity*." Donald laughed a little ruefully as he drew from his suitcase a slick-paper, sophisticated quarterly, aimed at high-brows and called *Trinity*.

In addition to publishing the magazine, Jean travels all around the country lecturing on the Baptism in the Holy Spirit and, when requested, praying with those who wish to receive it. She has a special way with the people for whom her magazine is edited: the well-educated, conservative suburbanite from the denominational church.

"These people do not approach the other areas of their lives excitably and demonstratively," she says, "and I don't see why the Holy Spirit should be presented to them under this guise."

We have heard her address groups and her presentation is very sane and quiet. "The apostles just assumed that Christians would receive the Baptism," she tells her listeners. " 'Have you received the Holy Spirit now that you have become believers?' they asked new converts. And if the answer was no, they entreated God to give Him to them at once, confident that God would not withhold this necessary power from any believer.

"I like being in this particular ministry," she often says. "It's the only one where you should expect one hundred per cent success. The Baptism is for the whole church. For every Christian."

Nor does she expect a great seizure of emotion at the moment of Baptism. "The new tongue is usually quiet and lovely," she says, "joyous but not frenzied." To Jean Stone receiving the Baptism is more like getting a kit of tools with which to do a job than an emotional experience. "It's a transaction between the Architect and his workmen. 'Will you work on this building of Mine? Here's the equipment you'll need.' And he provides us with healing, prophecy, wisdom, tongues, whatever we can use for our particular part in the construction."

But the Baptism is by no means always so tranquil. Dr. John F. Barton, a dentist in West Hartford, Connecticut, told me that his Baptism felt like receiving a massive jolt of electricity, painless but stimulating. Sometimes these jolts of power produce physical manifestations. A person's muscles may react, flexing and relaxing until he begins to shake all over. Or he may start to cry, or sing. Or he may literally be prostrated: the Holy Rollers, who are for the most part Negro Pentecostals, get their name from this unusual manifestation.

Physical reactions have defenders in unexpected quarters. I was surprised to read this in John Wesley's *Journal*:

The danger [wrote Wesley, talking of outcries, convulsions, dancing, visions, trances, and the like], was to regard them too little; to condemn them altogether; to imagine they had nothing of God in them, and were a hindrance to His work. Whereas the truth is:

(1) God suddenly and strongly convinced many that they were lost sinners, the natural consequences whereof were sudden outcries and strong bodily convulsions;

(2) to strengthen and encourage them that believe, and to make His work more apparent, He favored several of them with divine dreams, others with trances and visions;

(3) in some of these instances, after a time, nature mixed with grace;

(4) Satan likewise mimicked this work of God in order to discredit the whole work; and yet it is not wise to give up this part any more than to give up the whole. At first it was, doubtless, wholly from God. It is partly so at this day; and He will enable us to discern how far, in every case, the work is pure, and where it mixes or degenerates. The shadow is no disparagement of the substance, nor the counterfeit of the real diamond.

Physical manifestations are not the only possible response to the Baptism. There are also strong emotional reactions. In my correspondence there were constant references to a sense of well-being. Here are examples:

■ "It was like being flooded with joy."

■ "I started to praise God in the new language I had been given. There was at the same time a feeling that my spirit had taken wing; I was soaring heavenward on a poem."

■ "I started laughing. It was a strange thing to do, but I just wanted to laugh and laugh the way you do when you feel so good you just can't talk about it. I held my sides and laughed until I doubled over. Then I'd stop for a while and start again. Laughing. Laughing."

■ "For the first time I discovered for myself why the disciples were accused of being drunk at Pentecost. That's the way I felt at my own Pentecost: in the highest spirits. Just drunk with joy."

■ "With me there was peace. Just a wonderful, quiet, steady, deep peace."

Quite often, along with this sense of well-being goes some form of healing. One of the people we met at the "Saturday Group" in the Benjamin Franklin Hotel in Philadelphia was the wife of a Baptist minister who had an amazing story to tell. This lady had been born with one leg a full two inches shorter than the other and all her life had worn a built-up shoe on that foot. On the night she received her Baptism she felt a burning sensation in this leg, but paid no attention in the intense joy of the moment. Joy was her overriding reaction to the Baptism; she sat for hours on a sofa, tears of happiness streaming down her cheeks. But when at last she stood up to go home, she stumbled. The next step was the same. After she had tripped and hobbled the length of the room she realized what had happened. Her short leg had grown two inches:

the built-up shoe was making the legs unequal. The healing, she added that Saturday, looking down at two shapely shoes, was permanent.

The Reverend David C. Wilcox of Milwaukee, Wisconsin, had been advised by his doctor to take an ounce of brandy in hot water three times a day to relieve nervous tension. Six years later Mr. Wilcox was drinking a quart of vodka a day, swallowing box after box of lozenges in an effort to keep his alcoholism secret. He tried prayer, psychiatry, hypnotherapy, Alcoholics Anonymous—nothing helped him. Then one night he fell asleep on his knees after a long and intense prayer. When he awoke he knew that something immensely important was happening. He felt that the Holy Spirit was filling him with power. Specifically he knew that as of that instant he had completely overcome his problem with alcohol.

"God marvelously and miraculously delivered me from the demon of alcoholism," says Wilcox today, five years after his Baptism. "This deliverance came as quietly as the dew of the morning, and yet with such thunderous impact that it completely changed my life."

Another kind of healing frequently reported is a healing of the spirit. Marianne Brown of Parkesburg, Pennsylvania, is today a truly joyous person. She has a wonderful, infectious smile; but the lines around her eyes are not smile-lines: they come rather from the years Marianne spent as a chronic worrier.

Marianne lived in an eleven-room manse built back in the days when help was inexpensive and available. It was neither when the Browns moved into the house beside the old Presbyterian church. Marianne was constantly behind in her schedule: either she took care of the house and her five children and her minister-husband and neglected the needs of the parish, or else she helped with the parish work and the house suffered. Always late, always running, always under pressure,

Marianne grew steadily more desperate. Her solution was simple: when things got too bad she took to her bed.

"Those illnesses," Marianne told me one day when Tib and I were visiting her in Parkesburg, "brought a double reward: I got lots of sympathy and I was free from responsibility. Still, I knew this was no way to live. I knew that God had not intended for me to be a semi-invalid, but I was powerless to do anything about it."

And then Marianne received the Baptism in the Spirit. "The new tongue I was given," she said, "was intermingled with waves of mirth in which every fear I had just seemed to roll away. It was a tongue of laughter. And when I had finished laughing I felt that I would never again have to spend another day in bed because of worry." For eight years this prediction has proved true. "He lavished strength and joy on me, so that I was able to do in hours what before had taken days to accomplish."


Of all the variety of experience with the Holy Spirit, one thing held true in every case. Whether the Baptism came quietly or with a bang, unexpectedly or after long seeking, the ultimate result was to draw the individual closer to Christ. Jesus was no longer a figure on the pages of a history book. Nor, even, a memory from some personal mountain-top experience. His Spirit was with the Baptized believer in a present-time, minute-by-minute way, showing him at every turn the nature and personality of Christ.

And suddenly I realized that I had come full cycle.

This whole search had begun in the vacuum that had followed my own mountain-top experience in the hospital. I was following—perhaps all Christians follow—the path the disciples took: First, there was a direct, personal encounter with Christ. Then, He appears to go away. There is a longing for His return, and a helplessness, because nothing we do seems to to bring that return.

Wasn't the lesson I had learned from the Bible, and from the people who had had the experience today, that in order to see Him again we need the mediation of the Holy Spirit? "But when your Advocate has come, whom I will send you from the Father—the Spirit of truth that issues from the Father—he will bear witness to me." [8]

Chapter Eleven

# Room 405

There seems to be a strange link between taking a seemingly foolish step—which God specifies—and receiving spiritual power. Moses stretched his rod over the water at Jehovah's command and the Red Sea divided. The penniless widow was instructed, through Elisha, to collect many vessels and to start pouring oil into them from her small jar: when the widow had finished obeying she had collected enough oil to pay all her debts. Elijah had to strike the water with his mantle before it would part.

I once had occasion to talk about this phenomenon with Billy Graham. He had noticed it for years, and was of the opinion that the secret lay in overcoming self-consciousness and self-will sufficiently to perform the task. It was extremely difficult, he had found, for most people to get out of their seats and walk forward to the altar rail at one of his meetings. But he had also observed that the seemingly foolish gesture brought power with it.

For many people speaking in tongues falls into the same category. It seems to them pointless and embarrassing. In these people, no doubt, the final yielding of their tongues produces a deep religious experience. But this was not the point at which my own resistance came. I could see by now some of the logic behind tongues: I could imagine myself praising God in a language I could not understand; I could imagine myself praying for someone in tongues if I could not imagine how to pray for them with my understanding. By now, in fact, I was becoming increasingly eager to receive the Baptism in the Holy Spirit and it seemed fairly likely to me that tongues would be a part of it.

No, the point of resistance for me lay in a different quarter. There was one act which many of the Pentecostals performed which I was *not* going to do. They would stand up, raise both hands toward heaven, and shout "Praise the Lord!"

I knew that the practice was a very old one in the Judeo-Christian tradition:

> Because thy loving kindness is better than life,
> My lips shall praise thee.
> So will I bless thee while I live:
> I will lift up my hands in thy name.
> My soul shall be satisfied as with marrow and fatness;
> And my mouth shall praise thee with joyful lips.[1]

I knew that "Praise the Lord" was a favorite phrase of the psalmists, and was even part of the liturgy of my own well-mannered Episcopal service.

Nevertheless, the practice as the Pentecostals did it was objectionable to me. No doubt each person draws the line somewhere. . . .

December 2, 1960. It was the date of the opening of the Full Gospel Business Men's convention in Atlantic City to which Tib and I had agreed to go, back in the spring, so many months ago. The meetings were being held at The President, one of the large on-the-water hotels. Friday night we registered, went for a walk on the cold, moonlit beach and turned in early.

I don't know why I was so unprepared for the emotions of the breakfast meeting next morning. I'd been to many Pentecostal gatherings by now, but never to such a large one: early in the morning several hundred men and women crowded into The President's grand ballroom. They ate rapidly, then pushed their chairs back in obvious anticipation of something to follow.

On the platform at the end of the room sat two dozen business and professional men. Some, I was told, had flown across the country to attend the meetings; one had come in his own private plane.

While we were finishing our coffee, one of these men stood up and called out the name of a song. Everyone joined in, loud, lusty and wonderful as I'd heard it before among Pentecostals. By the middle of the second song a woman at the next table was weeping. There was nothing especially emotional about the song itself, it was one of the standard old Gospel hymns, "When I Survey That Wonderous Cross." But crying seems to be as infectious as laughter. Soon some of the men on the platform were unabashedly bringing out their handkerchiefs. What was it that swept a room this way? I felt it too; so did Tib sitting next to me. Both of us were studiously avoiding looking the other one in the eye.

As the music continued, several people at the tables began to sing "in the Spirit." Soon the whole room was singing a complicated harmony-without-score, created spontaneously. It was eerie but extraordinarily beautiful. The song leader was no longer trying to direct the music, but let the melodies create themselves: without prompting one quarter of the room would suddenly start to sing very loudly while others subsided. Harmonies and counterharmonies wove in and out of each other.

By now tears were flowing without restraint all around the room. A weathered, stonefaced man near us raised calloused hands and sang out, "Praise the Lord!" An elderly woman two tables away stood up and began to dance a little jig. She looked like a great grandmother, dressed in black with her white hair in a bun. No one paid her the slightest attention. Except me, that is; I couldn't take my eyes off her. And as I watched, a phenomenon occurred which I have still not been able to explain. It was very hot in the ballroom, perhaps 85 degrees. Yet while grandmother danced I distinctly saw, against the dark velvet curtains of the room, soft billows of visible "breath" coming from her mouth as if she were standing outside in the cold.

The effect on me of watching these manifestations is hard to describe. Instead of being embarrassed or feeling that I was watching something unseemly, I had the overall feeling that this was wholesome and good, and I remembered Dr. Van Dusen's remark that Pentecostal exuberance was "ultimately healthy."

And then suddenly it was all over. The singing stopped; the mood of the meeting shifted. People brought out handkerchiefs and dried their eyes. A California dairyman named Demos Shakarian, who is the Fellowship's president, stepped to the center of the platform and conducted the business end of the meeting. It was over in five minutes, and as the weary veteran of many treasurer's reports I was filled with gratitude.

A prayer followed. The "breakfast" meeting lasted for four hours. There was preaching and more singing. There was a period during which people from the floor could tell about some experience with the Holy Spirit. I noticed that several in the audience, when introducing themselves, confirmed what Charles Maurice had told us: there were others in the ballroom who were not Pentecostals by denomination, they were Episcopalians, Methodists, Baptists, Presbyterians, Lutherans. When at last the meeting adjourned for lunch, Dr. William Reed, a surgeon and an Episcopal lay reader whom we'd known for some years, came over to Tib and me and asked us to join a group who were having sandwiches sent to one of the rooms upstairs. The room they had chosen was to become strangely important to me: Room 405.

The door to Room 405 was slightly ajar when we arrived fifteen minutes later, so I knocked and we walked in, wondering who would be there. Sitting with his back to the window which framed the rolling, pounding Atlantic Ocean, was Jim Brown, a Presbyterian minister from Pennsylvania. Bill Reed was on the sofa, talking to a Methodist woman minister from Philadelphia, Olivia Henry. And out in the kitchen making coffee were an Episcopalian social worker named Dorothy Randall and Jim's wife, Marianne. There was not, I noted, a Pentecostal among us.

Tib sat down beside Jim with her back to the Atlantic. The conversation centered on the morning's meeting, the different people who had spoken, the points of view expressed. It was several minutes before I noticed that Tib was not joining in.

Sandwiches arrived from the coffee shop downstairs, and the talk turned to more personal subjects: the needs and hopes that each of us there in the room had brought to the convention. From time to time I looked across at Tib. She sat withdrawn and silent, the sandwich on her plate untouched. She'd said nothing about feeling bad that morning, but there was a weariness about her posture now—as though she held a tremendous weight on her shoulders, all alone.

All at once she stood up. She murmured something about having to make a phone call and before I could stop her, she was gone.

Something very strange was going on with all of this. Tib and I, alike in so many respects, were especially alike in one area. We were proud of our objectivity. We were then, and still are, of the opinion that objectivity and honesty are closely related. If you looked at a scene with many eyes, we believed, you were more likely to see it whole.

But objectivity also served another function for us: it acted as a shield. We were not by nature joiners or true-believers. We did not like to be identified with a group. And at the same time by profession and by instinct we really were interested in other people's enthusiasms. By keeping about us a spirit of objectivity, remaining always interested observers, but never committed participants, we were defended from the pressures of joining every group we wrote about.

I had made one major exception to this rule when I became a Christian. And with that experience I discovered a flaw in the principle of objectivity. Before I made my own commitment I thought of myself as viewing Christianity from as many vantage points as possible, thus getting an accurate view. What I did not realize was that this very objectivity was itself a block to seeing the whole picture. Because it effectively cut off one essential viewpoint: the view from the inside.

For many months now I had been looking at the Baptism in the Holy Spirit from as many angles as possible: all from the outside. I had decided with my intellect that this was a valid Christian experience. Now I wanted to explore it from the inside. Tib had followed most of the research and interviews. She was interested: but still only as an observer. I think now that when she left Room 405 she knew what she was doing. She was deliberately taking with her our burden of objectivity. She was making it possible for me to step inside an experience, taking defenses out the door with her.

Of course at the time I realized all of this only on the most subliminal of levels. I doubted that she had a telephone call to make; I knew that something was weighing on her; I sensed that she did not want me to follow her. In some mystic way she was to play a tremendous role in the event that followed, because she took with her our cherished outsider's look, while I was left free to participate in the shock and jolt of experience.

And yet leaving the room, she did not leave me, for we were mysteriously linked together during the next hours. When Tib left 405 she'd gone outside to walk on the boardwalk. After a while she stepped down onto the sand where she could walk right at the water's edge. She walked for a long, long time. The sun sank lower in the sky. Facing south as she was, her eyes began to be bothered by it. Tib has always been extremely light-sensitive, choosing chairs that looked away from windows and so forth. She started to turn around and head north with her back to the sun when a sentence popped into her mind with the force of a command.

"Look neither to the right nor to the left, but only straight ahead."

But straight ahead was the dazzling sun. She walked on a little farther, squinting her eyes. It was getting late. She was a long way from the hotel by now. The meeting in Room 405 must be over, she thought: I would be looking for her. But each time she started to turn around and retrace her steps, the extraordinary words reappeared in her mind.

"Neither right nor left. Only straight ahead."

The sun was lower still. Glittering on the waves, glaring straight into her eyes. And still Tib walked on, into the blinding light. . . .

In 405 there was a certain air of expectancy. There were six of us now, seated in a casual circle about the room. Several people had related instances of the power of Spirit-filled prayer, and someone now suggested that we pray this way for the problems on our minds.

Partly in an effort to overcome self-consciousness, I shut my eyes. Soon I'd lost track of who was talking in the room. Someone began to pray in the Spirit. It was a woman's voice, but I did not know whose. In fact, from that moment on I lost contact with individuals. It was as if the separate personalities had disappeared and a single individual, talking in various timbres and accents had taken their place. Minds seemed to work together: a sentence would be started by one person and finished by another.

Now someone else began to pray in tongues. Another started to sing very softly in the Spirit. I felt my throat tighten, as it had downstairs at the height of the singing. I suppose I was crying, deeply, silently. Slowly I began to lose my own identity too, until finally self-awareness disappeared.

This is quite an experience, losing consciousness of self. And I was helped by gaining, at the same time, the awareness that another Presence was in the room. And suddenly He was there again, in light as I had seen Him in the hospital. But this time the light blazed through my closed lids, blinding, dizzying, fearful. I was afraid of this approaching contact. I tried to pull my mind away from it, to concentrate on the solid room around me and the human beings in it.

"Look neither to the right nor to the left, but only straight ahead."

The voice came from behind me. I thought it was Olivia Henry's but I have never been sure. Just at the moment when I was about to take refuge in self-consciousness, it pulled me back to the center. Several times more, in the next hour, the command was repeated, always just in time to prevent my attention from being sidetracked. I never knew whether the words were meant for me or not, but they performed an immeasurable service. They kept me from being distracted by what was going on to either side, from being conscious of how I looked and what other people thought of me; they brought me back always to the blinding light directly ahead.

There was a lull in the praying and singing. The voices around me receded into a quiet murmur.

A man's voice: "I believe John wants the Baptism in the Spirit."

I felt, more than saw, the five people rise and form a circle around me.

What happened next is due in large part to the role Tib was playing as she walked alone up the beach toward the sun. I believe that, although I am unable to explain it. Without this help from her I would hardly have run the strange new danger of totally new experience.

At the time, there in Room 405, nothing of this was going through my mind. Just the opposite: the very nature of that hour was pure experience, with a maximum of allowing to happen what was going to happen, and a minimum of analysis.

The group moved closer around me. It was almost as if they were forming with their bodies a funnel through which was concentrated the flow of the Spirit that was pulsing through that room. It flowed into me as I sat there, listening to the Spirit-song around me. Now the tongues swelled to a crescendo, musical and lovely. I opened my mouth, wondering if I too could join in, but nothing happened.

I felt a numbness in my lips and a constriction in my throat.

And suddenly I had the impression that in order to speak in tongues I had only to look up. But this was a joyful gesture. All my training and inclination was to approach God with head bowed.

Strange that such a simple gesture as lifting the head should become a battleground. And soon—perhaps because I did not obey quick enough—another directive came clear: not only was I to lift my head but I was to lift my hands too, and I was to cry out with all the feeling in me a great shout of praise to God. A hot, angry flush rose and flooded me. It was the thing above all things that I didn't want to do.

Perhaps because it was so very repugnant to me the issue was clearly drawn as one of sheer obedience.

What other possible significance could there be in my raising my hands high and mouthing some words of praise? But that was what I had to do, and I knew it. Foolish as it seemed.

Or maybe because it seemed foolish. I heard E. Stanley Jones saying, "I had to become God's fool."

With a sudden burst of will I thrust my hands into the air, turned my face full upward, and at the top of my voice I shouted:

"Praise the Lord!"

It was the floodgate opened. From deep inside me, deeper than I knew voice could go, came a torrent of joyful sound. It was not beautiful, like the tongues around me. I had the impression that it was ugly: explosive and grunting. I didn't care. It was healing, it was forgiveness, it was love too deep for words and it burst from me in wordless sound. After that one shattering effort of will, my will was released, freed to soar into union with Him. No further conscious effort was required of me at all, not even choosing the syllables with which to express my joy. The syllables were all there, ready-formed for my use, more abundant than my earth-bound lips and tongue could give shape to.

It was not that I felt out of control of the situation: I had never felt more truly master of myself, more integrated and at peace with warring factions inside myself. I could stop the tongues at any instant, but who would? I wanted them never to stop. And so I prayed on, laughing and free, while the setting sun shone through the window, and the stars came out.

Chapter Twelve

# Through the Red Door

The next three months were one long smile, one long laugh, one long bounding out of bed each morning to meet the day. Never had I known such a protracted period of well-being. My work went well. I glimpsed what being a creative father could be like: when the children burst into my office I stopped working, really glad to see them, and when they left I turned back to the interrupted business without missing a beat. If one of the boys slipped into my shop and gouged a groove in my grinding wheel I bawled him out, sure, but in my annoyance was no rejection of him.

Many deep-rooted psychological quirks, which I had used most of my life to keep people at a safe distance, disappeared entirely during these months. I got to know old friends on an entirely different level and made new ones without the shyness which is my usual lot.

Bible reading moved into a new dimension. I discovered an interesting thing: you find in the Bible those Persons of the Godhead with whom you have had an encounter. For years I "saw" only the Father in the Scriptures. Then after the hospital experience I found the Son. And now it was the Holy Spirit. It was a phenomenal adventure, reading words I'd focused my eyes upon all my life yet never grasped. For the first time I approached the Gospels and Acts as descriptive rather than poetic writing. I read stories of miracles, demons, healings, spirits with brand new eyes.

Church, too, took on new meaning. For the first time I understood what the psalmist meant when he said, "I was glad when they said unto me, Let us go unto the house of the Lord." [1] I just liked being in church, the building itself, the congregation, the service. I remember that the Christmas communion seemed unusually brief to me. I commented on it to Tib, going out. She looked at me oddly. "We've been in here two hours," she said. And I, who'd always been Mr. Fidget himself, could have sat there another two.

I used my new tongue, too, during this period. There were two kinds of occasions when it seemed to come naturally. One was in response to beauty. I remember one January morning in particular when every twig on every tree was coated with ice. I looked out the bedroom window at this glittering world and it seemed the most natural thing in the world to express the indescribable in sound alone.

This experience began to occur fairly frequently. Something moving would happen, something which once might have sent a shiver up my spine, but now brought out the response of tongues instead. I recognized the phenomenon as a kind of wordless praise. It was praise which—in some mysterious way—allowed me to participate in the beauty, or the wholeness, or the majesty I had perceived. I found that the very response made me more sensitive to the situation which had called it forth, and I could imagine a person more experienced than I having a dozen such occasions every day, with each bringing from him this response of tongues.

The other times when I used them were in intercessions. I

remember praying in tongues one evening for a man in our parish whose wife had confided to us that her husband wasn't sleeping nights. That was all she said and since I scarcely knew the man it was useless to try to offer intelligent prayer for him.

At three o'clock that morning I woke up, stark awake, with the conviction that the man's problem was a long-standing resentment of one of the people where he worked, that he had never forgiven this other person for some ancient injury, and furthermore that I had to go and face him with the idea. I could not get back to sleep until I resolved to do it.

In the cold light of reason, the next day, this seemed a brash and presumptuous procedure. What possible excuse could I give for barging into a man's life with such a question? I tried to satisfy my promise—to whom I did not know—of the night before, by calling his secretary for an appointment, "some time at Bill's convenience." It didn't work. This very busy man had an hour open that same afternoon, and at three o'clock I was seated in his office afraid for my sanity.

"Bill," I said, "you'll have to forgive me if I'm wrong, but I've had the strangest feeling . . ." and then I explained to him the idea which had waked me.

When I finished Bill sat staring at his hands. I could hear his secretary typing out in the office. Her machine's end-bell rang four times before Bill spoke.

"How could you possibly have known?" he said.

Over the next two months Bill and I met once a week for lunch. I didn't talk very much. In fact I did little more than listen. But bit by bit the problem that Bill had been facing began to unravel itself, and in the process Bill came to have a new view of the Holy Spirit, because of course I had to tell him how I happened to call on him in the first place.

A more desperate problem was brought to my attention right in the middle of this when Tib rushed into my study one afternoon to say that the teen-age daughter of a very close friend had tried to commit suicide. She was on the hospital's critical list. Tib and I wanted to pray but had almost no information, not even how she had tried to take her life.

Again I used tongues, and I found myself recalling some words of Paul: "For if I pray in an unknown tongue, my spirit prayeth, but my understanding is unfruitful. What is it then? I will pray with the spirit, and I will pray with the understanding also. . . ." [2]

Paul wasn't claiming any great mystery here: he was just praying with another part of his makeup. He knew that he was in part rational man and as such should pray with logic. But he also functioned on a different level, a level having little to do with reason. Paul called this his spirit; today we might call it the unconscious or the subconscious. Paul rounded out his prayer life by allowing the deep, non-verbal side of his personality to pray too.

Wasn't this what I was doing in my prayer for this girl? I yearned for her health with my mind, but I yearned for her with my spirit too.

When we reached the hospital, she had been taken off the critical list. We drove her mother home and spent three hours with her. We could see that physical healing was just one corner of the prayer we could make for this family. The more we listened to the problem the more complex we saw that it was. Again, as it had been with Bill, our role was not one of counsellors: we wouldn't have known what to do or say. Our role was to keep the problem constantly in the framework of prayer, and in this I found tongues invaluable. They were like a protective screen around my own fallibility, keeping me from blundering into this life-and-death situation with my own opinions. As our friend talked I kept up a silent, continual petition in tongues for her, her estranged husband, their daughter. It was prayer, it was an avenue for God into the situation, but it by-passed the error-prone medium of my own mind.

But along with all these benefits of the Baptism, there was a drawback. The book. Here I was, midstream in what was intended to be an objective look at the current tongues movement, and I myself had become a no-holds-barred partisan. Inevitably, I watched the tone of the book change. I no longer wanted simply to describe: now I urged, I argued, I tried to persuade. There was nothing to do but lay the manuscript aside until I regained my sense of balance—or admitted that I had parted with it forever.

"Everyone," says Jean Stone, "has the right to be a fanatic for six months after his Baptism." I decided to give it longer still. Four years have passed now since that amazing afternoon in Atlantic City. Time, I think, has done some shaking down and proportioning for me, my views on this subject have recaptured, I hope, something of objectivity. Over this period one principal change has taken place in my attitude toward the Baptism in the Holy Spirit and toward speaking in tongues. With each year I have become less emotional about them; with each year I have become more convinced of their value.

This was by no means a simple, straight-line development. I have described the first flush of joy and wholeness following the Baptism as lasting three months. I'm not sure of the exact period, but after about that length of time, I had a sudden, violent reaction. It centered chiefly on tongues: I became suspicious that I was generating the whole thing. Indeed I often did mouth nonsense syllables in an effort to start the flow of prayer-in-tongues. But sometimes the easy, effortless flow never came. I'd be left listening to the sound of my own foolishness. It was obvious to me that the Holy Spirit was no part of these noises: the ridiculousness of it would sweep over me, and from there it was not far to wondering if the Holy Spirit had ever been a part of tongues.

Pentecostals became a stumbling block for me at this time too. Their exuberance had not seriously bothered me as long as I was outside looking in. But now I was inside, and what would others think if they looked in and saw me with these strange sorts? I remember attending a breakfast meeting of Pentecostals one morning where there was a photographer taking pictures for a magazine article. I spent an active meal trying to keep out of lens range.

It was fortunate for me that I'd been warned in advance about these reactions. The warning had come from Lydia. I'd written her about my Baptism and on her next trip to New York we met for lunch.

"Do you remember, John," she said, after hearing my story, "what the very first thing was that Christ did after He received the Holy Spirit?"

"He went into the wilderness, didn't he?" I said.

"More than that. No sooner had He been visited by the Holy Spirit than He was tempted by the devil. Has this happened to you yet?"

I put my fork down, interested. "Perhaps. Go on."

"You'll discover," said Lydia, "that once you meet the Spirit, you meet the devil too. It is a definite, certain fact that this onslaught is going to come. It happened to Christ, and the pattern still holds. The only thing you can do is be prepared for it."

The temptation, Lydia said, usually takes the form of doubt, perhaps doubt that the Spirit has really come. Or perhaps it shows itself as a reassertion of self-will and self-consciousness.

"It is no accident, this temptation," said Lydia. "I believe that the Holy Spirit deliberately allows it to happen. He wants you to use it. He wants you to cast a cold, rational eye over your experience. Then when you come out on the other side, the Baptism is yours not only as a gift, but also as a prize of battle."

I did have to battle doubt and pride, and other assailants of new-found health but I soon discovered that the fiercest enemies of the Spirit within are not these active sins but the passive ones: the sins of omission, indifference, inertia. I hadn't been familiar with the Holy Spirit for long before I knew that we are not made automatons by His presence. He will stay with us as long as we actively will it, work at it, yearn for His company.

One of the clearest indications of the fact that the Holy Spirit is a Person, and not some vague sort of automatic force, is the fact that He can indeed be grieved. "Do not grieve the Holy Spirit of God," said Paul.[3] I found that there are at least two ways we can grieve the Holy Spirit. One is by not being, in our inner life, good company for Him: He will simply go away for a while if He doesn't like the thought-company we are keeping. And the second is by neglect. The relation is like a friendship, in that it must be cultivated, exercised, enjoyed, if it is to last and grow.

I grieved the Spirit in both fashions and He drew off. But in the process I learned that I did not want to be without Him, and began to search for ways to invite Him back.

Thank God for the organized Church during this period. There it was, an institution, running along perhaps a little mechanically, but independent of the ups and downs of individual members of the congregation. We went each Sunday to church, and were aware that there was a steady consistent quality about the services that was important. Our particular church was not making many innovating experiments, but neither was it having to go through the cyclical swings of people who experiment. The church was *there*: solid, staid, formal, wonderful.

I found, too, that it was important to be regular about private prayer time during the week. Our friend, David Wilkerson, tithes his time in prayer. Twenty-four hours in the day; David prays for two and a half hours each day. I tried it. I broke the time into five units, early morning, mid-morning, lunch, early and late evening, half an hour at each of these times. The discipline is more than I can sustain, yet, but I know from the experiment that there is great power in the monastic idea of undergirding the day with regular periods of prayer. It was during the time of this experiment that I felt most consistently the presence and power of the Spirit.

I was not surprised, either, remembering my experience at the time of the Baptism itself, that obedience should also play a role in realizing the steady presence of the Holy Spirit. Here too I have glimpsed something bigger than I can yet achieve. What would it be like to live an entire day completely obedient to the will of the Spirit? Would His "still small voice" become clearer as time went on? I must work to cultivate a habit of listening for it.

What these four years have given me already, however, is a better understanding of what really went on in Room 405.

At the actual moment of the Baptism in the Holy Spirit, there was one overwhelming impression: I was bathed in, surrounded by, washed through with love.

I don't know why more hadn't been made of this in the things I had read on the subject. Perhaps because we are so concerned with the power-aspect of the Holy Spirit. But the nature of that power, I am convinced, is love. It was very like the love I experienced when I met Christ in the hospital room, except this was active, dynamic, propelling me to respond, while the love I encountered in the hospital was more of a quiet presence, demanding nothing.

Once I realized this, I had the answer to a riddle that had puzzled me. Throughout the New Testament the terms "Holy Spirit," "Spirit of Christ," and "Spirit of God" are used almost interchangeably. People who knew Christ and who knew the Holy Spirit obviously equated the two. "And they went through the region of Phrygia and Galatia, having been forbidden of the Holy Spirit to speak the word in Asia and when they were come over against Mysia, they assayed to

go into Bithynia; and the Spirit of Jesus suffered them not.
..." [4] "You are not in the flesh, you are in the Spirit, if the
Spirit of God really dwells in you. Anyone who does not have
the Spirit of Christ does not belong to him." [5]

The reason for this inter-exchange of persons was clear once
I had met the Holy Spirit. It was quite like meeting Christ.
And the common denominator was love. People who had met
Christ had had the experience of meeting love, and when these
same people met the Holy Spirit, they felt that they had had
another encounter with love. When they spoke about Christ's
Spirit interchangeably with the Holy Spirit they were doing,
instinctively, what theologians later did, logically: stating that
these were one and the same God. The only difference was
aspect.

There was a second puzzle which was answered by this discovery. There is a very old relationship in Christian thought
between the Holy Spirit and "sanctification." Paul speaks of
God who has ". . . from the beginning chosen you to salva-
tion through sanctification of the Spirit." [6] The classic cate-
chistic role of the Holy Spirit is God, ". . . who sanctifieth
me, and all the people of God." Wesleyan perfectionism and
its spiritual children, the various Holiness Movements of the
late 1800s, put emphasis on what was called the "second blessing," or the Baptism in the Holy Spirit, as an experience
which made men saintly.

The point is that there is a very old idea that the Holy
Spirit is functioning in our lives not only to give us power as
Christians, but also to clean up our lives, lead us toward holiness. I will have to admit that certain kinds of holy Christians
have always repelled me. I have never been able to tell
whether it is because they make me uncomfortable, knowing
that I am far from holy; or whether they are in fact making a
serious error in supposing themselves to be holy when in fact
all they are is sanctimonious. I will have to admit also, how-

ever, that I have met a few Christians who make no show of
holiness yet whom I sense to be living on a different plane
from my own. These people have a quality which strikes me
as being at the heart of real holiness; they do not make me
aware of their goodness so much as of their hope. They do not
point up my shortcomings in contrast to their saintliness, they
point up my potential.

I think Christ must have had this kind of holiness. He
would never have attracted men like rough Peter and worldly
Matthew otherwise. The secret ingredient in this kind of
transforming holiness, I came to think, was love. When I
came into contact with love as an overwhelming experience in
the Baptism in the Holy Spirit, I found that I had been
cleansed, built up, healed. I knew a kind of wholeness I'd
never dreamed of: and the words whole, holy and health are
all derivatives of the same Anglo-Saxon word *hāl*, meaning
complete. This is the type of sanctification that comes from
contact with the Christ-love of the Holy Spirit.

There is another result of this contact. E. Stanley Jones,
when he received the Baptism of the Holy Spirit on the campus of Asbury College, changed from being a student of
Christianity into a teacher of it.

"It was then I learned the difference between a disciple and
an apostle," he told me. "One is passive, the other active. A
disciple is a man who sits at Christ's feet. An apostle is a man
who goes out for Christ into the world: a missionary, if you
will; although a missionary doesn't have to go any further
away from home than next door. The point is that it is this
experience of the Baptism in the Holy Spirit which translates
the passive into the active."

It must be this way. I saw it in my own experience. The
episode with Bill—going to see him about his problems, even
caring enough to say a prayer for him in the first place—was

completly out of character for the kind of person I'd always been. And this was only one of many such instances. I, self-centered, introverted, preoccupied with my own problems, suddenly found myself going out of my way to know other people, really caring about them, really wanting to help. And as soon as anyone does that, of course, the possibilities for being used are endless. Within two years of the experience in Atlantic City, Tib and I found ourselves in Africa with our three children on a year's assignment, teaching, living, working with a tribe of people we'd never even heard of.

Dr. Frank Laubach's experience with the Holy Ghost turned him around and sent him out to become the world's greatest literacy teacher. This is how he accounts for the phenomenon.

When Christ was here on earth [Dr. Laubach says], He was limited to performing His ministry in one place and at one time. He was one man, walking beside one sea in one little corner of the earth. He healed whatever He touched, but His touch was necessarily limited by time and by space.

Now, does it make sense that the Father would send His Son for this limited ministry? I don't think that is tenable. He made provision to carry on the work through the Holy Spirit: *we* are to complete His mission. We are His multiplied hands, His feet, His voice and compassionate heart. Imperfect and partial to be sure, but His healing Body just the same. And it is through the Holy Spirit (Christ's love which is everywhere at once), that we receive the power to carry on the work of apostles. It is a challenging and sobering thought: when we receive the Holy Spirit into our lives, we receive the same urgent and life-giving force that led our Master.

It seems to be a psychological fact of human nature that in order to give, we must first receive. "We love, because He first loved us," says John.[7] But it is also true that once we have received this love there is an equally compelling need to give it away. Indeed, we sense instinctively that this is the only way we can keep it.

The Baptism in the Holy Spirit is the gift of love such as we have never known it. The natural aftermath is to be propelled forward by the power of this overflowing love into the world, seeking opportunities to share the thing that has come to us.

# Wedding the Old to the New

But how are we to share this thing, in terms of the actual town where we live and the church where we go?

In my case—and I think it is typical—it seemed to me there were three possibilities:

(1) To stay in my church, preaching the Pentecostal experience.

(2) To leave my church and join a Pentecostal group.

(3) To stay in my church, say nothing about this other experience, and keep company with Pentecostals on the side.

The choice was not a simple one. My little Episcopal church, settled in one of the rather conservative suburbs of New York, was typical of most in that very few members had heard much about the Baptism in the Holy Spirit. They'd heard a lot about tongues. Through headlines and magazine articles, they knew that all over the United States these odd goings-on were upsetting things. And probably most of them were saying to themselves: I hope it doesn't happen here.

Time and again I had watched the tensions that were created when a member of one of the traditional churches received the Baptism and then returned to his parish. Here he came, walking on springs, eager to share this wonderful thing that had happened to him. He forgot, perhaps, that he himself had gone through a slow evolution in viewpoint from cautious skepticism about the Pentecostal experience, to full-flood belief. Far too often in his enthusiasm he forgot basic strategy, and instead of being able to communicate, his very boldness blocked his ability to reach others.

Furthermore, another effect of the Baptism can create problems. The Baptism in the Holy Spirit is an enormously invigorating religious experience: it fills people with energy. If this energy cannot be channeled into constructive areas, it is likely to spend itself in a kind of frenetic running-around. I'd known Spirit-filled people who were constantly boarding jet planes to rush about the country on various missions for the Holy Spirit. This kind of undirected hyper-activity never failed to strike me both as heroic and as sad: heroic because the individual really did give of his time and substance—plane fare is expensive—and sad because the expenditure ended up, somehow, egocentric.

Then there was a curious problem created by the fact that the Pentecostal really is an effective Christian. While his enthusiasm scares some, it attracts others and soon there is a division within the church between those who are pro-Pentecostal and those who are not.

In the end I chose the third path: I returned quietly to my church, spoke about my experience only when it came up naturally, and kept company with my Pentecostal friends elsewhere.

Yet, this is not a good solution either. If I believe in the importance of the Baptism in the Holy Spirit, as I do, do I not have an obligation to talk about it wherever and whenever I can?

This is the problem which faces many thousands of Americans today, as the Pentecostal movement spreads. As things stand, it is irresolvable. As things stand, the Pentecostal experience does not fit readily into the life of the traditional churches.

But isn't it possible to change things?

The suggestions I am making assume that it is. They look to the day when this seeming conflict can become instead a constructive dialogue between freedom and order, youth and maturity, each immeasurably the richer. To bring this day about, there are things all of us can do.

For those of us who have had the Baptism of the Spirit:

Let's look carefully—even thankfully—at the criticisms which are leveled against us. They can be of immense value in helping us to use well this overwhelming gift of God.

Let's pay special attention to the question of timing. We have a tendency, I think, to be impatient—as if the course of Pentecost depended upon us and not upon Christ. The Baptism is His to give, and any forcing or rushing on our part can only come from a lack of perspective, or a lack of faith. Or even lack of humility, should we ever be tempted to chalk one up for our side.

Let's remember that the gifts of the Spirit were given "to build up the church," [1] and not for the private use of individuals. Everything we are given must be accepted with this understanding if we are to avoid forming little cliques of "elite" who see themselves as separate from the rest of the Church. The Church's weaknesses and her strengths are ours: ours are hers.

Let's look at our use of tongues in the same light. In favor of the practice, it is interesting to note the Sponsors' List of tongues, as it were. It includes: the Mother of Jesus, Peter, James, John, Andrew, Philip, Thomas, Bartholomew, Matthew and Paul.

And yet this same Paul saw clearly the dangers in undisciplined use of tongues. He set down explicit instructions on how they were to be used, where, by whom and for what purpose, instructions that all of us who use tongues would do well to re-read from time to time.

Let us be more concerned with "the harvest of the Spirit" in our lives. This harvest as detailed in Galatians 5 is: love, joy, peace, patience, kindness, goodness, fidelity, gentleness, and self-control. What kind of personality would this combination of qualities produce? An other-centered, quietly forceful, humble, listening, confident yet empathetic man, who is filled with joy. Is this a description of the Pentecostal? Often, yes. And when it is, he is a walking advertisement for the experience. It isn't a description of me, however, which says to me that the Baptism in the Holy Spirit is the open door to new life, but not the new life wrapped up and delivered.

Let's look again at the function of structure in religion. For most of us, the discovery of spontaneity in worship was a life-giving revelation and we become anxious when someone suggests imposing a pre-decided order on Spirit-filled prayer meetings. But are we forgetting that pattern is essential in all true growth? If growing things had only energy without plan, we would never see such end products as an oak tree or a human being or a full spiritual life.

And now some suggestions for churchgoers who have not had this experience.

None of us wants to be part of a passing fad, any more than we want to stand aside while a great move of God is taking place. I suppose, with Gamaliel, an ideal attitude would be ". . . if this work be of men, it will come to naught; but if it be of God, ye cannot overthrow it, lest haply ye be found even to fight against God." [2]

Who is right, those who say the Pentecostals are on the far-out fringe of religion, or those, like Dr. Van Dusen of Union, who feel they are part of the central thrust of our times? The question is so important that churches are increasingly spending time and money on depth reports of Pentecostal activity in their areas.

As for the disruptive effects of this activity on a congregation, the very qualities that bring the disruption are the ones most churches pray for. The Pentecostal importunes us with his message, but who hasn't felt that his own witness is a little tepid? The Spirit-filled man may be too ebullient for comfort, but who hasn't wondered a little wistfully if more joy in belief isn't the Christian's birthright? He wears us down with his energy, but who hasn't wondered what became of early Christian vigor?

If these are all qualities any church would want, where does the trouble come from?

First of all, I think, from the fact that the Holy Ghost has become in many church traditions, ever more ghost-like and shadowy, so that we are genuinely unprepared for initiative on His part. We have made an abstraction out of the most powerful Person on earth, and the encounter with the reality is going to be a shock.

Then there is the fact that any minister wants and ought to be the leader of his own Christian community. And here from outside comes an experience which parishioners tell him is the religious turning point of their lives. But in these ecumenical days the solution is not far to seek: it lies in seeing ourselves as members of the larger Church, as well as of our own congregation or denomination. What on one scale is an experience coming in from outside, on another scale is simply the shared experience of the Church.

And then, of course, there is the stumbling block of tongues, so abnormal, so often the first characteristic encountered. It may help to know that nine-tenths of the distaste people feel is often simple unfamiliarity. During our stay in Africa, Tib and I had the unusual opportunity of meeting men and women who can remember when they heard the

Christian story for the very first time. What a shock to them was the idea of God nailed to a cross, or born in a manger, or suffering hunger! Uncouth, inappropriate, unlovely—all the adjectives we ourselves had applied to tongues—they used for this strange Gospel. And it's certainly true that tongues, once the strangeness has worn off, are not unpleasant to listen to—in fact are often extremely beautiful.

If the Pentecostal experience occurs in your church, why not—while you're making up your mind about it—put it to work? Do floors need scrubbing? Has that cracked sidewalk been repaired? I know many Pentecostals who are performing just such tasks in their churches and finding them an outlet for overflowing energy.

The Pentecostals claim new power in prayer. Why not make some experiments to find out? Give the Pentecostals among you a specific prayer-task. When one church in New York put on a membership drive recently, Pentecostals in the congregation took it in turns to pray around the clock. Could this have had anything to do with the spectacular success of the drive?

And witnessing. Christ linked this with the Baptism: ". . . ye shall receive power after that the Holy Ghost is come upon you: and ye shall be witnesses unto me. . . ." Why not let your Pentecostals take a part in the witnessing work of the church. And I'm not talking about witnessing to the experience of Pentecost. Christ did not say, ". . . ye shall be witnesses to the Baptism in the Holy Spirit." It is never the function of the Spirit to call attention to Himself. The Baptism is nothing more than a means to an end, and the end is always Christ.

What about the ill in the church? I am constantly being impressed with the close relationship between the Baptism and the power to heal. I know two Massachusetts women, Judy Sorrenson and Kay Anderson, who are frequently called upon by their Episcopal priest to minister the healing gifts given to them with the Baptism. In Chicago a Spirit-filled Baptist minister is known to the chaplains of several hospitals as a man whose prayers bring results. Perhaps power like this is available in your church.

The whole point is to suggest that Pentecostals can be integrated into the real work and real needs of any church. And most Pentecostals go about such work—when it is welcomed, needed, and properly channeled—quietly and tactfully.

This does not mean that such service within a traditional church will satisfy all of *his* needs. The Pentecostal has discovered in his free, Spirit-led worship something of infinite value, and all the Spirit-filled people I know who have stayed in their old denominations, also meet regularly outside them —on Wednesday nights or Saturdays mornings or only once a month—for this other kind of service from which they draw such strength.

And I suggest that this need of the Pentecostal is everyone's need, part of universal human nature which requires both order and freedom. Most of us handle this split in our needs by keeping order in our religious life and leaving freedom to ball games and political rallies. But here is a description of a Temple service in Jerusalem:

> O praise God in his sanctuary . . .
> Praise him in the sound of the trumpet: praise
>     him upon the lute and harp.
> Praise him in the timbrels and dances; praise
>     him upon the strings and pipe.
> Praise him upon the well-tuned cymbals: praise
>     him upon the loud cymbals.
> Let everything that hath breath praise the Lord.[3]

In virtually all religions before the modern era this exuberance was an integral part of worship. While in Africa, we went to the opening of the Anglican cathedral in Mbale, Uganda. After a stately formal service inside the new building, some of the same people came outside, rolled out the tribal drums and plunged into a dance of thanksgiving and triumph which was unmistakably worship—and impossible to listen to without tapping feet and clapping hands. This side of us is going to come out somewhere: it is religion's loss if it is confined always to the secular.

And I am continually surprised at how welcome freedom-in-worship is among the people I consider conservative. We recently lured one of our older neighbors into a Pentecostal midweek service. There was a good deal of just plain noise: clapping, shouting, lusty singing, and I looked over a bit apprehensively to see how he was taking it. To my amazement he was clapping his hands with the best of them. He caught my look and called out over the heads in between: "Why not?" Why not indeed? We need freedom and we need structure. The traditional churches have emphasized the one, the Pentecostals the other. Is there any way to combine the two?

In Parkesburg, Pennsylvania, a farming community near Lancaster, there is a beautiful old Presbyterian church where the balance has been struck in a way that might well become a pattern in many churches. Every Saturday night the church holds a Pray and Praise service. A band led by the pastor's son provides the music. There are spontaneous prayers, intercessions and thanksgivings from the congregation. Presbyterians, Methodists, Baptists, Episcopalians, as well as Pentecostals come from as far away as Washington, D.C., to pack the basement auditorium in a service that lasts far into the night.

Then Sunday comes. The eleven o'clock service is everything a beautiful tradition can make it. For decorum you could not tell it from any other Presbyterian service—except perhaps that the pews are a little more tightly packed, the singing more spirited, the preaching unusually inspired.

Here is a church where order and freedom have both been welcomed, and both made stronger. Not long ago I talked with Dr. John Alexander Mackay, president-emeritus of

Princeton Seminary and one of the country's leading theologians.

"If it is a choice," he told me, "between the uncouth life of the Pentecostals and the aesthetic death of the older churches, I for one chose uncouth life."

But what if there need not be this choice? What if there can be a synthesis on a higher plane than either, so that in our churches we have form and life growing Godward together? What if Pentecost comes to the Church today?

# References

*Sources*

NENT: New English Bible, New Testament. Copyrighted 1961 by The Delegates of the Oxford University Press and The Syndics of the Cambridge University Press, and used by permission.
ASV: American Standard Version
RSV: Revised Standard Version of the Bible. Copyrighted 1946 and 1952.
Where no translation is specified, see the King James Version.

CHAPTER ONE
1. John 3:2 (NENT)          2. John 3:3 (NENT)

CHAPTER TWO
1. 1 Cor. 14:26-28; 39-40 (RSV)

CHAPTER THREE
1. *Life* magazine, June 6, 1958.

CHAPTER FOUR
1. Mark 1:7, 8
2. Acts 1:4, 5 (NENT)
3. Acts 2:1-4 (NENT)
4. Acts 2:4
5. Acts 8:14-19
6. Acts 9:17, 18
7. Acts 10:44-47
8. Acts 19:1-6
9. 1 Cor. 14:18
10. Cincinnati *Inquirer*, Dateline Jan. 27, 1904, Galena, Kansas.

CHAPTER FIVE

1. *World Dominion*, April, 1932, quoted by Donald Gee in *The Pentecostal Movement* (Elim Publishing Co., Ltd., London, 1941).

2. *Like a Mighty Army* by Charles W. Conn (Church of God Publishing House, Cleveland, Tenn., 1955).

3. Ibid.

CHAPTER SIX

1. Abridged excerpts from an editorial in *The Living Church*, July 17, 1960.

2. From *The Episcopalian*, May 15, 1963.

3. On the occasion of the opening of the 1961–62 seminary year at Princeton.

4. From *The Rule of God* by G. Ernest Wright (Doubleday & Co., Inc., New York, 1960).

5. From a message to the Sacramento, California, ministerium, as reported in the January, 1961, issue of *Full Gospel Men's Voice*.

6. Dr. Philip E. Hughes in an editorial in *The Churchman*, September, 1962.

7. *The Catholic Messenger*, Davenport, Iowa, Nov. 7, 1963.

8. Reprinted with permission from *America*, the National Catholic Weekly Review, 920 Broadway, New York, N.Y., 10010.

CHAPTER SEVEN

1. Mark 16:17
2. Acts 10:45, 46 (NENT)
3. Acts 2:4 (NENT)
4. Acts 11:15
5. 1 Cor. 12:7, 10 (RSV)
6. 1 Cor. 12:28 (RSV)
7. 1 Cor. 12:8–10 (ASV)
8. 1 Cor. 12:7 (NENT)
9. 1 Cor. 14:4 (ASV)
10. 1 Cor. 14:26 (RSV)
11. 1 Cor. 12:28 (RSV)
12. 1 Cor. 14:14 (ASV)
13. 1 Cor. 14:16 (NENT)
14. Romans 8:26 (NENT)
15. 1 Cor. 14:18 (ASV)
16. 1 Cor. 14:15 (ASV)
17. 1 Cor. 14:2 (RSV)
18. 1 Cor. 12:30 (ASV)
19. 1 Cor. 14:5 (ASV)
20. 1 Cor. 14:39 (ASV)

CHAPTER EIGHT

1. *Trinity* magazine, Vol. III, No. 1.
2. *Trinity* magazine, Vol. II, No. 2.
3. 1 Cor. 14:4
4. Romans 8:26, 27
5. Romans 8:26, 27 (NENT)

CHAPTER NINE

1. 1 Cor. 14:2 (RSV)
2. Acts 2:4, 6–8, 11
3. Mark 13:11

CHAPTER TEN

1. Psalm 51:10, 11 (ASV)
2. Psalm 139:1, 5, 7 (ASV)
3. Isaiah 11:1–2 (ASV)
4. Isaiah 42:1 (ASV)

5. John 3:5 (ASV)
6. Luke 24:49 (ASV)

7. John 3:8
8. John 15:26 (NENT)

CHAPTER ELEVEN

1. Psalm 63:3–5 (ASV)

CHAPTER TWELVE

1. Psalm 122:1
2. 1 Cor. 14:14–15 (ASV)
3. Ephesians 4:30
4. Acts 16:7 (ASV)

5. Romans 8:9 (RSV)
6. II Thess. 2:13
7. I John 4:19

EPILOGUE

1. 1 Cor. 14:27 (NENT)
2. Acts 5:39

3. Psalm 150 (ASV)

# OTHER HIGHLAND BOOKS

Here are the first titles from Highland Books, launched in 1983 by Edward England, former Religious Publishing Director of Hodder and Stoughton, to reprint modern Christian classics.

# THE ADVENTURE OF LIVING

*Paul Tournier*

Dr Paul Tournier, now retired, was a general practitioner in Geneva for nearly fifty years. Here he explains that God guides us when we are on the way, not when we are standing still, just as one cannot steer a car unless it is moving.

'Despite our uncertainties and our vagueness, even through our failings and mistakes... He leads us step by step, from event to event.'

'The Bible gives adventure its true meaning, for from end to end it reveals what is at stake in all our work, all our activity, all our choices, and all our self-commitment.'

# ESCAPE FROM LONELINESS

*Paul Tournier*

'It is our own secrets that separate us the most from others; remorse for our wrongdoings, fears that haunt us.'

# A DOCTOR'S CASEBOOK IN THE LIGHT OF THE BIBLE

*Paul Tournier*

'Our profession is a priestly ministry. I should like to see the church consecrating doctors just as it ordains ministers. This would be in conformity with the gospel. It is the conviction which makes us give ourselves with our hearts and minds and souls to our vocation.'

'A work of the deepest spiritual insight.'

*Church Times*

# SECRETS

*Paul Tournier*

'Keeping a secret is the first step in becoming an individual. Telling it is the second step.'

'An exceptional man indeed, of faith, dedication and sympathy.'

*Bishop of Llandaff*

# MARRIAGE DIFFICULTIES

*Paul Tournier*

'You have problems? That's quite normal; all couples do. As a matter of fact it is a good thing. Those who make a success of their marriage are those who tackle their problems together and who overcome them. Those who lack the courage to do this are the ones whose marriage is a failure.'

# WHAT IS A FAMILY?

*Edith Schaeffer*

In an age when the family is being threatened as never before, Edith Schaeffer presents a powerful reaffirmation of the joys of family life. She writes as wife, mother and grandmother at L'Abri, the Christian community in Switzerland.

# EVANGELISM IN THE EARLY CHURCH

*Michael Green*

Canon Michael Green is both an evangelist and a New Testament scholar. This has enabled him to produce one of the finest books on this subject ever written.

'Expert... a most lucid examination.'

*Daily Telegraph*